LITERACY & LEARNING CENTERS

Content Area and Disciplinary Literacy Tools for Grades 4-12
Volume 1

Katherine S. McKnight, Ph.D.

Edited by Elaine Carlson
Front Cover design, layout and additional graphics by Kris Lantzy

Printed in China

First Printing May 2019

Published by Engaging Learners, LLC
Antioch, IL

Visit EngagingLearners.com

For Ellie and Colin, my children,
who teach me lessons every day.

TESTIMONIALS

"Dr. Katie McKnight has really knocked it out of the park! Energize your secondary and middle school student readers with these easy-to-implement and engaging learning stations. **Students deserve and need this kind of "hands-on and minds-on" learning** to become more independent learners. Now is the time to diversify student experiences and let the lively sounds of activity ring out in your classroom. This new book is an invaluable tool for time-strapped teachers with limited resources."

Dr. Kathy Perez,
Professor Emerita Saint Mary's College of California, international consultant, author

"If you teach any content area and ELA skills in grades 4–12, you must use Dr. McKnight's Literacy & Learning Center model in your classroom on a regular basis. Not only does McKnight provide research to support how this way of teaching improves engagement and literacy among students, but she also produces action research from some of this nation's most struggling schools to demonstrate that it works *quickly*! **To support your implementation, this book gives step-by-step directions, examples, and samples** – and even an amazing book list organized by themes. Get your whole school on board and watch your literacy scores soar!"

LeAnn Nickelsen,
Maximize Learning, Inc.,
Atlanta, GA

"Wow! This is a book for all the teachers who have questioned *how* to increase content-area **literacy (while also keeping students motivated and engaged)**, as well as, *what* materials and resources are needed to ensure student success. Dr. McKnight's LLC model is easy to implement in today's classrooms and the activities provided are sure to keep the students engaged."

Melissa Dickson,
Professional development presenter, teacher coach, and educator

"As a high school reading teacher of many below grade level readers, I find it is sometimes difficult to find strategies to engage my students. Although my students *can* read, they often have difficulty connecting with texts in a meaningful way so that they can effectively read to learn. **Literacy & Learning Centers have been a game-changer for my students,** not only in their interactions with texts, but by causing their reading comprehension and overall classroom achievement to increase exponentially! The practical ideas and easy-to-adapt tools in this book will transform your classroom experience."

Elizabeth Knost,
High School ELA teacher,
Anderson Community School Corporation,
Anderson, IN

"Differentiation in a middle school or secondary setting is difficult. Knowing how to manage it has been something that I, and the teachers I support, struggle with. The tools and examples in this book provide **the perfect guide to actually differentiate effectively.** I wish this book had existed years ago!"

Brenna Sherwood,
Middle School Instructional Facilitator
Farmington Municipal Schools, Title 1
Farmington, NM

"In the process of improving learning outcomes for students, one often hears that 'the joy has been removed from teaching.' Becoming adept at utilizing Literacy & Learning Centers in your classroom **will return the joy, raise test scores, and most importantly, increase student engagement.** Dr. McKnight has created a road map for Literacy & Learning Centers that is simple to follow but rich in results."

Julie Mitchell, MA, Ed. S.,
Reading Specialist & School Advocate,
Resource Training & Solutions:
Regional Centers of Excellence,
Central Lakes Region, MN

"Leave it to Dr. Katie McKnight to once again offer up a relevant, easy-to-use, 'how-to' book for teachers who want to **support and improve student literacy for 4th–12th graders**. McKnight's experience in using literacy centers to differentiate and teach important content is sure to make an impact on classrooms across the country. The bulk of the book contains specific examples of mini-lessons that including great features such as prep time, clear instructions, and ideas for adjusting the rigor. As a literacy teacher, when I want great lesson ideas, I know that I can always turn to Dr. McKnight's books for effective ideas I can easily adapt for my classroom in centers or as mini-lessons to benefit my students. Two big thumbs up!"

Daniel M. Argentar,
Communication Arts Instructor/Literacy Coach,
Adlai E. Stevenson High School,
Lincolnshire, IL

"One of the must have guides for any educator wanting to implement Literacy & Learning Centers in the classroom! **Jam-packed with honesty, strategies, lessons, and materials**, Katie McKnight delivers what all 21st century content-area teachers need to be successful and confident in literacy development. *Literacy & Learning Centers: Classroom Tools for Grades 4-12, Volume 1* will make grade 4–12 educators fearless incorporating centers into their classrooms. 'Knowledge is Power and Literacy is the Path.'"

Elizabeth (Libby) Perry,
Data/Literacy Coach,
Anderson Elementary School,
Anderson, IN

"Dr. McKnight has done it again! With her 18th book, *Literacy & Learning Centers: Content Area and Disciplinary Literacy Tools for Grades 4-12, Volume 1* she has written yet **another masterpiece for classroom teachers**. In her 2017 book, *Literacy and Learning Centers for the Big Kids, Grades 4-12*, she made the case that the utilization of leaning centers toward literacy development simply works, as evidenced via her **100% success rate in achieving academic gains** with her unique, centers-based approach. In this new book, she further expounds on the learning center model for teaching literacy. It's an essential tool for any teacher of students in grades 4–12."

Principal Baruti Kafele,
Highly regarded author, speaker,
urban educator and school leadership expert

"Dr. McKnight has found **the balance between content learning and the critical need for older students to develop their literacy skills**. The research-based Literacy & Learning Centers model (LLC) allows for highly effective independent and small group center-based activities that actually cover more discipline-specific content in less time and in a more effective manner than the traditional 'sit and get.' Not only does this book explain the LLC model, the sample center activities include approximate prep time and set-up information. It also includes copy-machine-ready sample center instructions, graphic organizers, and more. If you read this book at home tonight, you will want to start using centers in your classroom tomorrow."

Lisa Hollihan Allen,
6-12 Literacy Intervention/Title 1,
West De Pere School District, WI

"Katie McKnight's work is always grounded in two things: reality and research. **The way she breaks sophisticated theory and research into practical and doable steps for teachers translates into real results for students**. See the schools in Farmington, NM if you need an example. I have been learning for over a decade from McKnight and see how her flexible learning model translates into blended learning models, across grade levels, and into the practices of content area teachers in all kinds of districts. This book's chapters are concise enough to read in one brief sitting at a time, and the examples are so concrete, they can be implemented immediately."

Eileen Murphy,
Founder & CEO of ThinkCERCA

"Thank goodness for Katie McKnight! She has added another wonderful resource to her extensive collection for teachers of struggling and reluctant adolescent readers. By focusing on building students' background knowledge and vocabulary, McKnight delivers a practical Literacy & Learning Center model that **can be implemented in any classroom**."

Danny Brassell, Ph.D.,
Internationally acclaimed speaker,
bestselling author, and co-creator of
ReadBETTERin67Steps.com

ACKNOWLEDGMENTS

With all projects like writing a book, there are numerous people to thank and recognize. I would like to thank the many teachers who graciously allowed me to access their classrooms to co-teach, observe, and problem solve as we worked together to ensure that all children are engaged in dynamic and powerful learning.

Elaine Carlson, the goddess of all things administrative is integral in all aspects of my professional work, including this book. If you call the Engaging Learners office, her pleasant demeanor is always on the other line. Kris Lantzy designed the cover, layout, graphics, and illustrations. I am lucky to know so many talented professionals.

ABOUT THE AUTHOR

Dr. Katherine McKnight is a dynamic presenter, dedicated teacher, and award-winning author. She began her career in education over 30 years ago as a middle school and high school English and social studies teacher in the Chicago Public Schools. In addition to speaking at professional development conferences, she is a regular consultant in schools and classrooms in the United States and Europe.

Dr. McKnight has served as a Distinguished Professor of Research at National Louis University. She is the founder of Engaging Learners, an educational company built around her successful Literacy & Learning Center model. Her work in educational leadership, literacy and student skill development has resulted in unprecedented academic achievement in many struggling schools.

Katie has received several awards for her publications and teaching at the university level. She has authored 18 books that support educational strategies to engage all learners. Her titles include the best-selling *The Teacher's Big Book of Graphic Organizers*, winner of the 2013 Teachers' Choice Award. She's also written *The Second City Guide to Improv in the Classroom*, *Teaching Writing in the Inclusive Classroom*, *The Teacher's Big Book of Graphic Organizers: 100 Reproducible Organizers that Help Kids with Reading, Writing, and the Content Areas*, *Literacy and Learning Centers for the Big Kids: Building Literacy Skills and Content Knowledge* and *Strategies to Support Struggling Adolescent Readers*.

TABLE OF CONTENTS

Chapter 1

_ _ _ _ _ _ _ _ _ _ _ _ _ _

Why Content- and Discipline-Based Literacy Matters

Why Content- and Discipline-Based Literacy Matters

You and I probably share a bond. I authored this book to provide the critical information and resources for teachers of older students; you picked up this book to support the development of your students' literacy. We want the same: for *all* students to develop the literacy skills they need so that they can have a successful future – a future in which they will read and comprehend texts as well as write and speak competently about what they know and understand. You and I realize these skills are essential, regardless of whether our students are in an ELA class or in a content-area classroom. And I don't think we're alone.

The reality is, the National Assessment for Educational Progress (NAEP) consistently documents the lack of improvement and proficiency for American students in grades 4, 8, and 12. In fact, according to test results, the majority of our students are not proficient readers. The results are even more concerning for students of poverty. (Wexler, 2018)

As discipline-specific teachers, our academic call for our students is two-fold: to develop their content knowledge, and to strengthen their literary skills. Yet many teacher preparation programs, especially for teachers of older students (grades 4–12), don't include coursework to develop student literacy skills. Let me use myself as an example. As a high school teacher, I didn't learn about the highly complex process of literacy skill development until I earned two graduate degrees in reading. I cringe when I think of the lost

opportunities to help my students and what I could have done during my early years of teaching if only I had known how.

It's not news to anyone in the education field that, nationwide, we've been struggling to find a balance between content learning and literacy skill development. Schools have historically organized curricula around specific subjects and academic disciplines (Sizer, 2004). Consequently, it's easy for us to lose focus in directly teaching literacy skills within the disciplines. In many ways, this practice has put us at odds with the requirements of legislative educational policies such as No Child Left Behind and its replacement, Every Student Succeeds. Although there are differences between these policies for general K-12 education, they have much in common. In both, significant emphasis has been placed on student reading performance.

Under both policies, schools were required to administer reading tests with penalties if higher scores were not achieved. In the nearly two decades since No Child Left Behind was enacted, many schools increased reading instruction at the cost of reducing or eliminating subjects such as social studies, arts, the humanities – even sciences. The message was clear: mastery of reading skills is so important that it must take precedence over content learning. So why hasn't reading performance improved?

Cognitive scientists have known for decades that simply mastering comprehension skills doesn't ensure a young students will be able to apply them to whatever texts they're confronted with on standardized tests and in their studies later in life. (Wexler, 2018)

Daniel Willingham, a cognitive psychologist who has long studied the science of reading comprehension documents that, "Whether or not readers understand a text depends far more on how much background knowledge and vocabulary they have relating to the topic than on how much they've practiced reading comprehension skills" (Wexler, 2018). Background knowledge is critical, and it's why students need to delve into a variety of subjects and disciplines. In short, if literacy comprehension is going to improve, our students need experiences with texts from a wide variety of subjects.

Willingham and others assert that in order to increase reading comprehension, students must expand their background knowledge and vocabulary. How do we do that? We teach our students social studies, science, and the arts while exposing them to a wide variety of texts and digital media. Even the oft-discussed achievement gap in reading performance can largely be attributed to students' lack of exposure to rich and challenging curricula and a range of disciplines.

Adolescent Literacy is Different

Regardless of where I work, in schools all over the United States and Internationally, literacy performance, especially in reading, significantly decreases in grades 4 and 5. What happens in these middle grades? As Chall's research documents (2000), there is a critical transition point at which students begin *reading* to learn as opposed to *learning* to read. This transition typically happens around 4th or 5th grade and it is what makes adolescent literacy different.

Most teachers of 4th-12th graders are able to cite many examples of instances in which their students were able to decode text but were unable to comprehend it. The simple decoding of words and recalling basic information of a text are characteristic of the *learning to read* phase. Yet, as students progress through school, they are exposed to more complex ideas and more detailed information through discipline specific texts. Exposure to these texts, as well as related digital media, is essential so that students not only learn content, but also learn to analyze information and develop new ideas and understandings. Students are expected to *read texts to learn* about the disciplines. Adolescent students do this at varying degrees as they march through a regimented schedule, jumping from one discipline to the next. This results in the greatest challenge: how do we ensure that students are developing literacy skills in all subjects in order to ensure their academic success in a variety of situations?

Going beyond the textbook is a good way to provide students with a wide variety of content and discipline specific texts while promoting background knowledge and vocabulary development. However, it is important to note, that there is debate among reading experts as to whether this is the best way to accomplish this goal. According to Shanahan (in Wexler, 2018), there is no evidence that providing differentiated reading improves student reading. He explains that students benefit more from reading texts that are harder and at respective grade levels. In light of this assertion, I ask that you to consider the work of another key reading researcher, Richard Allington. In *Every Child, Every Day*, Allington and his co-author, Gabriel (2012) explain that each student must read something he or she understands. They explain,

Understanding what you've read is the goal of reading. But too often, struggling readers get interventions that focus on basic skills in isolation, rather than on reading connected text for meaning. This common misuse of intervention time often arises from a grave misinterpretation of what we know about reading difficulties. (Allington and Gabriel, 2012)

It makes sense that adolescent readers should be given plenty of opportunity to practice with texts that they can read accurately, fluently, and with understanding. In addition to providing exposure to background knowledge and seeing vocabulary words in context, accessible texts give readers an opportunity to build reading "muscle memory." Fluency necessitates practice. It can be thought of as the bridge from decoding to comprehension. As teachers, developing content knowledge and reading fluency is essential. (McKnight and Allen, 2018)

Literacy & Learning Centers are Different, Too

As Jensen and Nickelsen explain in their 2008 book, *Deeper Learning: 7 Powerful Strategies for In-Depth and Longer-Lasting Learning*, use of cooperative learning groups leads to a host of positive outcomes. It improves everyday decision-making ability and emotional intelligence status, as well as helping to develop students' cognitive abilities and working memory. And the results will be even more pronounced if it happens in all classes, not just English Language Arts.

ENGAGING™ LEARNERS

The concept of content literacy has been around for a long time – and it's been a hotly debated topic of discussion for at least the past 30 years. The question has always been: how can content-area teachers – teachers of science, history, mathematics and the like – integrate literacy development into their classrooms? As I stated earlier, we've grown accustomed to thinking that education is compartmentalized and that literacy skills are the special purview of ELA teachers. And, as content area teachers are quick to point out, they never seem to have enough time to cover their own material, let alone worry about students' literacy skill development.

With the Literacy & Learning Center model, teachers actually *cover more content in less time*. When combined with ample independent and small group reading, this center model is an ideal way to teach content *while developing student literacy skills*.

Don't have time to figure out how to do it yourself? Need specific ideas? My years of direct work with classroom teachers have revealed a demand for tools for teachers like you to use as-is in your classroom Literacy & Learning Centers. As educators, we all need activities that can easily be adapted to meet the specific needs of our class, whether we teach science, social studies, humanities, mathematics, literature, technical and life-skill classes – or even PE. So introduce your students to high-level literacy development activities, like those included in this book, and provide them ample opportunity for independent or small group reading. It will quickly become obvious that it is possible to teach your content and develop student literacy skills simultaneously. There are many ways to develop and practice literacy skills, and the LLC model is effective. We'll explore that in the next chapter.

Preparing Students for College, Career, and "The Test"

And lest you be concerned that by incorporating Literacy & Learning Centers you won't adequately prepare your students for college and career – or even worse, that you won't prepare them for your state's standardized test – rest assured. When students are engaged in center-based activities, they are actually *doing more to prepare, not less*.

Frequent and long lectures, sometimes referred to as "sit and get," cause our students to become disengaged and bored. They aren't learning or retaining information and they aren't developing skills. That doesn't help with college, career, or test taking, and it no longer reflects what students can expect to encounter beyond high school.

Unlike the lecture hall experiences I remember from my collegiate years, long lectures that don't engage students are no longer the norm in higher education. In addition to being an experienced high school teacher, I was a tenured professor for fifteen years at two different universities, so I've witnessed this firsthand. Universities are now preparing students for 21st century careers that require collaboration, creative problem solving and innovation. Typical undergraduate assignments include things like working in teams to create projects and portfolios – exactly the tasks they'll do in the workplace. When high school and middle school students work in centers, they are actually honing the skills that will be in demand in the workplace and in college. They're learning how to apply what they know and demonstrate their understanding of content.

Because standardized tests are so important to school districts throughout the country, let me repeat something I've said many times before: good teaching always takes care of testing. Always. When students are engaged in meaningful work in centers they learn how to be more independent, confident, knowledgeable and competent. In every district where I have implemented the Literacy & Learning Center model, student performance and proficiency goes up. There's quite a bit of evidence out there, too, that if we keep purchasing test prep books and prepare students to take "the test," overall student performance goes down. So why would we keep throwing money at a problem if it doesn't improve the results?

Knowledge is power and literacy is the path. The right to read and write was once reserved for only a segment of the population. Yet in the 21st century there is more demand on literacy than ever before. We have tremendous access to information and our ability to find, understand, and evaluate written text requires intellectual dexterity and speed. The survival of our democracy is dependent upon its citizens' abilities to discern the credibility and determine the importance of a wide range of information. Middle school and high school are the best places to practice and develop that vital literacy.

Notes
_____
_____
_____
_____
_____
_____
_____
_____
_____
_____
_____
_____
_____
_____
_____
_____
_____
_____
_____
_____
_____

References

Allington, R., & Gabriel, R. (2012). Every child, every day. *Educational Leadership*, 69(6), 10-15.

Chall, J. S. (2000). *The academic achievement challenge: What really works in the classroom?* New York: Guilford Press.

Jensen, E. and Nickelsen, L. (2008). *Deeper learning: 7 powerful strategies for in-depth and longer-lasting learning.* Thousand Oaks, CA: Corwin Press.

McKnight, K. S. and Allen, L. H. (2018). *Strategies to support struggling adolescent readers, grades 6-12.* Lanham, MD: Rowman & Littlefield Publishers.

Sizer, T. R. (2004). *Horace's compromise: The dilemma of the American high school.* New York: Mariner Books
.

Wexler, N. (2018, April 13). Why America Students Haven't Gotten Better at Reading in 20 Years. Retrieved from *The Atlantic*: https://www.theatlantic.com/education/archive/2018/04/-american-students-reading/557915/

Notes on this Chapter

Chapter 2

- - - - - - - - - - - - -

Why the Literacy & Learning Center Model is the Solution

Why the Literacy & Learning Center Model is the Solution

The Literacy & Learning Center (LLC) model grew out of research-based theories about the most effective practices for the development of literacy skills and content knowledge. It's not a program that schools purchase; it's a method for using resources that teachers and students already possess or can easily acquire.

The LLC model aligns with several pedagogical approaches, including:

- Gradual Release of Responsibility
- Growth Mindset and Self-Regulation
- Formative Assessment
- Differentiated Instruction
- Multi-Tiered System of Support (MTSS)

And because the LLC model was developed through collaboration with classroom teachers in schools all over the United States and internationally, it works in all kinds of classrooms and with all kinds of students. It has proven effective in school districts. And everywhere it has been employed, districts have seen amazing growth in student literacy. It's not hyperbole when I say, "With Literacy & Learning Centers, students achieve two years of measured literacy skill growth in just one year."

For example, Mesa View Middle School in Farmington, NM was a Title I school that was struggling to raise performance.

They implemented the LLC model, coupled with a proficiency scale based assessment initiative, over a two-year period. In those two years, Mesa View's state report card skyrocketed from an "F" school to a "B." Their sister school, Hermosa Middle School, witnessed similar gains. In the same two-year period, that school's state report card rose from a "D" to a "B."

East St. Louis, a city in southwestern Illinois, was featured in Jonathan Kozol's seminal work, *Savage Inequalities: Children in America's Schools*. Once a bustling industrial center, by the late 20th century the region was mired in extreme poverty. Skip ahead to 2014 when, as a result of the local school board's search for new and innovative instructional methods, School District 189 adopted the Literacy & Learning Center model for their middle school and high school students. After the teachers and I implemented the model, for the first time in decades, middle school and high school students in East St. Louis demonstrated increased performance on the Northwest Evaluation Association Measures of Academic Progress (NWEA) test. My East St. Louis colleagues and I were encouraged and excited to learn that the students' proficiency levels increased over 15% in two years.

Stories like this are amazing but, as it's important to note, they're not isolated examples. They've come to be expected. And because the LLC model actually increases student engagement and teacher empowerment, the positive results continue growing long after the initial implementation.

Literacy & Learning Centers Overview

As educators, we need to resign ourselves to the reality that we will never have enough time to do everything we are tasked to do. That's just a fact. However, in the last decade, hundreds of teachers have discovered that they are able to cover more content in less time through center-based instruction. The model isn't complicated or difficult to use. All it requires is some preparation and a game plan.

When most teachers think of learning centers, they think of K-3 classrooms. While that's certainly a useful application, the early elementary classroom isn't the only place learning centers can be used to build literacy skills and content knowledge. I've used them in middle schools and high schools, with gifted students, high-poverty students, students with special needs, ethnically diverse students, and English language learners. Experience has shown that *all* students actually tend to be more engaged when they work in centers. The combination of self-directed activity and short, specific task lends itself to the natural strengths of the developing adolescent. Students with special needs, in particular, report that they feel "safer" in these small groups. They are often able to learn from and with their peers while finding it easier to concentrate – especially in inclusive classrooms. Teachers find that learning centers enable them to cover more content and skill development in the same amount of class time. Plus it's easy to give individual attention and personalized instruction to students who need it.

Concise Description of Literacy & Learning Centers

The teacher presents a short mini-lesson that focuses on a single instructional "chunk" of information, content, or literacy skill. Often this is followed by a brief activity in which the whole class reviews concepts and practices skills that were taught during the mini-lesson. Then small teams of students rotate through stations. At each station they are presented with a short, specific activity that, (1) gives them an opportunity to practice, review, and/or apply the skill or content that was taught during the mini-lesson, (2) they complete with some level of cooperation, and (3) offers them some small choice in how they proceed with the activity.

Foundational Centers

I recommend that you start with four foundational centers which are the concentrated source from which literacy skills are nurtured and developed: Reading Together, Vocabulary, Writer's Craft, and Teacher-Led Center. A fifth center, Grammar, gives students a valuable opportunity to work together in applying the rules of Standard English to all content areas in organic, real-world ways. A Speaking & Listening center is usually the next one added to the rotation, because spoken literacy is a natural outgrowth of reading and writing. It provides obvious opportunities for reaching struggling communicators and expanding literacy for all students. Other content-specific centers that include practical applications can easily be added after these foundational skills are addressed.

Reading Together Center

We know that once students develop skills in decoding and fluency, the simple act of reading more text improves comprehension. And research indicates that truly exemplary teachers differentiate instruction so that all students have access to texts they can actually read fluently and accurately (Allington, 2002). We also know that providing students with choices in their reading makes a big difference in motivation.

Incorporating Literacy & Learning Centers into the classroom is a great way to accomplish this. Giving students time to read and explore text during the classroom in built in to the Reading Together center. And by giving adolescents an opportunity to choose their reading material, you'll greatly increase the chance that they'll actually read it. Providing choice doesn't mean that students can select just any text. Choice means that we, as educators, provide more than one text for students to select. In doing so, not only can we increase motivation, but we can also appeal to students of various interests and ability levels.

Allow students to be grouped by choice. In this way, each student in the class will personally select the text that most interests them, and will be placed in a group with the other students who picked the same text. Allowing students to be grouped by choice provides a dramatic boost to student motivation.

ENGAGING™ LEARNERS

Because this concept may be new to many teachers, Chapter 3 includes classroom-tested examples of differentiated reading lists for a range of classrooms and content areas. I invite you to borrow heavily from these lists or to use them as inspiration to create your own lists.

Chapter 4 is comprised of activities and tools that aid students in developing their reading comprehension. As they make their way through middle and high school, students encounter more and more complex texts. These tools can be modeled in a mini-lesson and then included in a center rotation for additional practice.

Vocabulary Center
According to my teaching colleagues, vocabulary presents the greatest challenge to student comprehension – more than any other aspect of reading. Ironically, thanks to ample research, we now know that asking your students to copy words and definitions is the *least* effective way to teach new vocabulary. Substantial research in this area (Marzano & Pickering, 2005; Coxhead, 2006; Fisher & Frey 2014) provides the following recommendations for effective vocabulary instruction:

- Limit the number of vocabulary words to 12–15 per list.
- Students must practice with the new vocabulary (a minimum of five times) in order to foster comprehension and usage.
- Teach vocabulary in context.
  To put it another way, students need to understand how words are connected. Providing long lists of vocabulary words that are not connected to current content area study is *not* an effective technique.

Look to Chapter 5 for examples of tools which provide students with engaging opportunities to actually work with content-area and academic vocabulary in context.

Writer's Craft Center
In the last thirty or so years, we have benefitted from writing gurus such as Lucy Calkins, Don Murray, Tom Romano and George Hillocks. The work of these experts and many others have established that students develop writing skills when they:

- Write often
- Rethink and revise their writing
- Talk about their writing
- Work together as a community of writers, and
- Recognize the importance of expressing what they know and understand through writing.

In the Writer's Craft center, students work on writing skills that are applicable to the content area being studied. As you examine the tools in Chapter 6 you'll notice that they include opportunities for students to practice skills that will be needed to produce longer texts, as well as plan for future routine writing activities – all with an eye toward various tasks, purposes, and audiences.

Teacher-Led Center

The teams of students meet with their teacher in this dedicated center. It presents an excellent opportunity for teachers to provide descriptive feedback and work one-on-one with each student. As we know from extensive research in assessment and grading (Heritage, 2010; Popham, 2005, 2011), providing immediate descriptive feedback about student work is critical for continued growth and achievement. Depending on the progress students have made, the teacher may use this center to provide support to students who need additional help, reinforce a particular skill for the benefit of the group, or provide enrichment opportunities to academically achieving students.

Additional Centers

Grammar Center

Grammar isn't just for ELA teachers. Everyone – from scientists to sportscasters, from music critics to construction foremen – all need to be able to effectively communicate. And effective communication requires an understanding of how thoughts are put into sentences and how sentences are properly constructed. That's why this center is a valuable addition to the content area classroom: it reminds students of the importance of clearly expressed communication in all subject areas.

Check out Chapter 7 for tools that will make it easy to reinforce understanding of grammar while students learn your content. They'll differentiate between sentences and sentence fragments, identify parts of speech, reinforce their understanding of punctuation, explore sound-alike words, and practice speaking in complete sentences.

Speaking & Listening Center

A lot of educators refer to speaking and listening as the forgotten aspects of literacy. We spend so much time teaching students how to read that we forget they also need to learn how to listen intelligently. We focus on writing, and yet often overlook the necessity of well-composed, spoken communication.

We find, that students need to discuss what they're learning when students discuss their reading, writing, and learning, they are more likely to retain it. Students have been shown to benefit from listening to a fluent adult read aloud (Skinner, Oliver, Hale, & Ziegler, 2006; Rasinski et al., 2005). So it is important to bear in mind that hearing a passage can be just as educationally valuable as reading it. By having your students listen to oral presentations or audio content, you can provide important background for the texts being studied. Look at the tools in Chapter 8 for activities that will give students a chance to identify a speaker's claim and evidence, explore a speaker's reasoning, and participate in their own argumentation.

How to Use this Book

I discovered in my work with teachers that one of their most pressing needs was a source for LLC activities, particularly for foundational centers. Although the vast majority of teachers already have a plethora of resources that can easily be adapted to Literacy & Learning Centers, they wanted specific instructions and ideas to help get started. That is the purpose of this book.

As you explore the tools and look at the sample booklists, keep in mind they are only suggestions. They're here to help you formulate a plan that will work in *your* classroom, with *your* students. All of the tools can be adapted. In fact, the majority of them were the result of teachers like you, adapting

ENGAGING™ LEARNERS

their old quizzes, worksheets, and lesson plans to this new, engaging model. So feel free to tweak! If you encounter something that works well, please reach out and let me know. As teachers, we are our own best resource. I'd love to help you share your discoveries with others.

And please don't think that you can only use these activities with the LLC model. Most of the strategies in this book can be easily adapted for use on days when you're not using centers. Feel free to present a mini-lesson and then have your students complete the associated activity as a full-class, as partners, or even independently. It's vitally important that we give students plenty of opportunity to practice key literacy skill development, so squeeze it in whenever and wherever you can. It's especially valuable in the content area classroom. Content study - whether the content is social studies, science, humanities, technology, or whatever – provides an amazing array of occasions for students to work on their literacy skills in authentic situations.

This book's description of the LLC model has been intentionally brief. I assume that you, dear reader and fellow educator, want to get to the activities so that you can start adapting them for your very own classroom. If you want to learn more about the model, detailed instructions and support for implementation can be found in my book, *Literacy and Learning Centers for the Big Kids, Grades 4-12* and on the Engaging Learners website, **engaginglearners.com/literacy-learning-centers**. I even have a team of Engaging Learners professional development experts available to travel to schools and districts to offer hands-on assistance and support teachers as they discover opportunities to use centers to combine literacy development with content learning in every class – even math! To learn more, please visit: **engaginglearners.com**.

Notes

References

Allington, R. L. (2002). What I've learned about effective reading instruction from a decade of studying exemplary elementary classroom teachers. *Phi Delta Kappan, 83*(10), 740-747.

Coxhead, A. (2006). *Essentials of teaching academic vocabulary*. Boston, MA: Houghton Mifflin Company.

Fisher, D., & Frey, N. (2014). Content area vocabulary learning. *The Reading Teacher, 67*(8), 594-599.

Heritage, M. (2010). *Formative assessment: Making it happen in the classroom*. Thousand Oaks, CA: Corwin Press.

Kozol, J. (1991). *Savage inequalities: children in America's schools*. New York, NY, Harper Perennial.

Marzano, R. J., & Pickering, D. J. (2005). *Building academic vocabulary: Teacher's manual*. Alexandria, VA: Association for Supervision and Curriculum Development.

Popham, W. J. (2005). *Classroom assessment: What teachers need to know (4th edition)*. Boston, MA: Pearson/Allyn and Bacon.

Popham, W. J. (2011). *Transformative assessment in action: An inside look at applying the process*. Alexandria, VA: Association for Supervision and Curriculum Development.

Rasinski, T. V., Padak, N. D., McKeon, C. A., Wilfong, L. G., Friedauer, J. A., & Heim, P. (2005). Is reading fluency a key for successful high school reading? *Journal of Adolescent & Adult Literacy, 49*(1), 22-27.

Skinner, C. H., Winn, B. D., Oliver, R., Hale, A. D., Ziegler, M. The effects of listening while reading and repeated reading on the reading fluency of adult learners. *Journal of Adolescent & Adult Literacy*.

ENGAGING™ LEARNERS

Chapter 3

Selecting Books for Text Complexity

PREP TIME

It's fairly easy to replace one reading assignment with a differentiated list in about 1 hour. Allow 4 or more hours to craft reading lists for an entire unit of study.

Selecting Books for Text Complexity
Grades 4-12

Explanation of Reading Lists

Literacy & Learning Centers require you to divide your students into small groups. I recommend that you group students not based on ability, but based on the texts they choose. In other words, each student selects the text that most interests him/her, and is placed in a group with the other students who picked the same text. This doesn't mean anything goes! The teacher or curriculum director should supply a selection of texts that all address the same basic literary themes, cover the same content, or address the same essential question. I call this selection of texts a *Reading List*.

How to Compile Differentiated Reading Lists

All classrooms and student readers are different, so there is no magic formula to creating the perfect list. Here's the process I suggest.

Step 1
Determine your objectives.
Is your class going to explore an essential question? Do your students have to be exposed to certain content? Write a list of "must haves" and then write a wish list.

Finally, make a note of your required text complexity range. Look at the example from a 7th grade science teacher on the next page.

ENGAGING™ LEARNERS

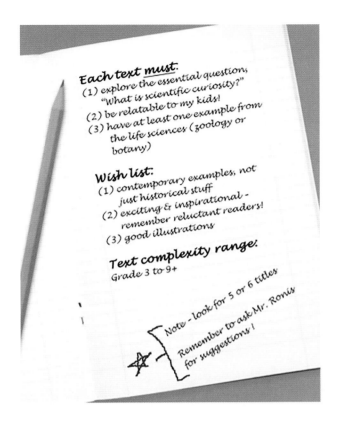

Each text must:
(1) explore the essential question,
"What is scientific curiosity?"
(2) be relatable to my kids!
(3) have at least one example from
the life sciences (zoology or
botany)

Wish list:
(1) contemporary examples, not
just historical stuff
(2) exciting & inspirational -
remember reluctant readers!
(3) good illustrations

Text complexity range:
Grade 3 to 9+

Note - look for 5 or 6 titles
Remember to ask Mr. Ronis
for suggestions!

Step 2
Explore your options.
This is the most time consuming part. Ideally you'll consider a lot of texts. Work with a school librarian, share ideas with other teachers (in your school and from outside groups), and seek out advice from reputable critics and book sellers.

Flexible Grouping and Text Complexity

First, consider these two truths: students will generally pick texts that they can under-stand; and students are more motivated to read challenging texts when they choose the text themselves. Oftentimes teachers are inclined to consider texts based only on standardized test data. But that data relies generally on the quantitative measures of a text. It's important to remember that the three components of the text complexity model are synergistically equal.

The Text Complexity Model has three equal components. Choosing which texts to include in your class reading lists means you must do more than consider quantitative measures!

The three components to consider are:

1. Quantitative Measures
These factors are difficult or impossible for a person to evaluate efficiently so they are typically measured by computer software. Examples of quantitative measures include students' standardized test scores and a book's assigned Lexile® scores.

2. Qualitative Dimensions
These characteristics must be evaluated by a teacher. They include considering levels of meaning (for literary texts) or purpose (for informational texts), as well as structure, language conventionality and clarity, and knowledge demands.

3. Reader and Task Considerations
This component is best evaluated by a teacher like you, who understands his or her students. It requires assessing the reader's motivation, knowledge, and experiences, as well as assessing the purpose and complexity of a text.

Unlike Lexile or Accelerated Reader scores, text complexity is generally represented in grade bands, When you look for texts, consider grade bands such as 3rd-5th grade, 6-8th grade, 9-10th grade, or 11-12th grade. And realize that it's not unusual for classrooms to include readers that fit in more than one band. For example, a 6th grade teacher might have student readers that are comfortable reading texts in the 3rd-5th grade band, and a few students who are ready for the 9-10th grade band.

Essential Questions are big questions that require students to explore, reflect, and are not easily answered. Focusing your curriculum around essential questions frees you to offer your students exciting, innovative lesson plans, center activities, and texts. For more information about essential questions, read *Understanding by Design* by Grant Wiggins and Jay McTighe.

Of course you can still offer your students a choice of reading material even if your school's curriculum is not centered around essential questions. Simply look for texts that cover your content while meeting different levels of the text complexity model. Be creative when looking for sources. Check out your school library, websites (like the Smithsonian, National Wildlife Federation, Brittanica Kids, etc.), trade journals, magazines, or even newspapers. In biology, if the objective is to encourage students to explore examples of "good bacteria", for example, you can find relevant texts in many places. An ELA teacher reviewing literary devices can consider many texts that incorporate similies, personification, metaphors, etc

Reading Lists: More Than Books!

Do you teach in a content area which rarely includes novels or full-length books in the curriculum? You could replace a textbook reading assignment with a reading list of short articles (online or in print). This is a great way for any teacher to get started with differentiated reading lists, or to incorporate them more frequently into the classroom.

Teacher Tips

If you've never offered students a choice of reading before, start small. Replace one reading assignment with a menu of reading options. I promise, when you see the difference in student engagement and motivation, you'll do it again and again!

Coming up with reading lists is an ongoing process. As you find new titles, as your school's curriculum changes, and as student interests evolve, it's likely you'll want to make revisions and adjustments.

Explore the **engaginglearners.com/literacy -learning-centers** resources website for other resources about differentiated reading (webinars, tips, etc.) to help you create your own reading lists.

Notes

_____

_____

_____

_____

_____

_____

_____

_____

_____

_____

_____

_____

ENGAGING™ LEARNERS

Grade 4 Sample Reading Lists

Topic: Cause and Effect

Essential Question: Is it usually possible to find the one most important reason that something has happened?

TEXT COMPLEXITY	BOOK TITLE	AUTHOR
2nd-5th grade	The Magic School Bus And The Climate Challenge	Joanna Cole
2nd-6th grade	The Tragic Tale of the Great Auk	Jan Thornhill
4th-8th grade	Fields of Fury: The American Civil War	James M. McPherson
2nd-6th grade	Ballet for Martha: Making Appalachian Spring	Jan Greenberg and Sandra Jordan
4th-8th grade	Hello World!: Computer Programming for Kids and Other Beginners	Warren Sande and Carter Sande
2nd-4th grade	DK findout! Coding	DK
3rd-7th grade	A Crooked Kind of Perfect	Linda Urban
4th-8th grade	Holes	Louis Sachar
3rd-5th grade	Satchmo's Blues	Alan Schroeder
4th-7th grade	When You Reach Me	Rebecca Stead

Topic: Building a Community

Essential Question: How do we get over disagreements with the people on our team?

TEXT COMPLEXITY	BOOK TITLE	AUTHOR
4th-6th grade	Friends of Liberty	Beatrice Gormley
4th-7th grade	Mossflower	Brian Jacques
1st-4th grade	Ant Cities	Arthur Dorros
4th-7th grade	Life on Surtsey: Iceland's Upstart Island	Loree Griffin Burns
3rd-6th grade	Charlotte's Web	E.B. White
4th-8th grade	Fault Lines in the Constitution: The Framers, Their Fights, and the Flaws that Affect Us Today	Cynthia Levinson and Sanford Levinson
2nd-5th grade	Seeds of Change: Wangari's Gift to the World	Jen Fullerton Johnson
4th-8th grade	The City of Ember	Jeanne DuPrau
2nd-4th grade	Sugar Hill: Harlem's Historic Neighborhood	Carole Boston Weatherford
3rd-6th grade	Somos como las nubes / We Are Like the Clouds	Jorge Agrieta

Grade 4 Sample Reading Lists

Topic: Investigation

Essential Question: How can we be more sure that something we learn is the truth?

TEXT COMPLEXITY	BOOK TITLE	AUTHOR
3rd-7th grade	Encyclopedia Brown, Boy Detective	Donald J. Sobol
3rd-6th grade	The Great Shelby Holmes	Elizabeth Eulberg
3rd-6th grade	12 Great Moments That Changed Newspaper History	Lori Fromowitz
1st-4th grade	The Daring Nellie Bly: America's Star Reporter	Bonnie Christensen
4th-7th grade	Why Is Milk White?: & 200 Other Curious Chemistry Questions	Alexa Coelho and Simon Quellen Field
1st-4th grade	Erosion: Changing Earth's Surface	Robin Koontz
4th-8th grade	The Revealers	Doug Wilhelm
3rd-7th grade	Chasing Vermeer	Blue Balliett
4th-8th grade	The Way Things Work Now	David Macaulay
1st-4th grade	Thomas Edison and His Bright Idea	Patricia Brennan Demuth

Topic: Natural Wonders

Essential Question: What do we learn from traveling in nature?

TEXT COMPLEXITY	BOOK TITLE	AUTHOR
3rd-6th grade	Wildwood	Colin Meloy
3rd-7th grade	Volcanoes and Earthquakes	Ken Rubin
3rd-7th grade	Child's Introduction to the Night Sky: The Story of the Stars, Planets, and Constellations-and How You Can Find Them in the Sky	Michael Driscoll
4th-8th grade	The Dreamer	Pam Munoz Ryan
1st-4th grade	Queen of the Falls	Chris Van Allsburg
4th-7th grade	Voyage of the Dawn Treader	C.S. Lewis
3rd-6th grade	The Penderwicks: A Summer Tale of Four Sisters, Two Rabbits, and a Very Interesting Boy	Jeanne Birdsall
3rd-7th grade	Beyond the Sea of Ice: The Voyages of Henry Hudson	Joan Goodman
3rd-5th grade	Cody Unplugged	Betsy Duffey

Grade 4 Sample Reading Lists

Topic: Cultural Exchange

Essential Question: How does learning from others help build trusting relationships?

TEXT COMPLEXITY	BOOK TITLE	AUTHOR
Kindergarten-4th grade	Corn Is Maize: The Gift of the Indians	Aliki
3rd-5th grade	The Silk Route: 7,000 Miles of History	John S. Major
3rd-7th grade	Maximilian and the Lucha Libre Club	Xavier Garza
4th-7th grade	Cool Architecture: Filled with Fantastic Facts for Kids of All Ages	Simon Armstrong
4th-8th grade	The Inquisitor's Tale: Or, The Three Magical Children and Their Holy Dog	Adam Gidwitz
1st-4th grade	One Green Apple	Eve Bunting
3rd-5th grade	Out of My Mind	Sharon Draper
3rd-7th grade	Ambassador	William Alexander
4th-8th grade	The Birchbark House	Louise Erdrich
1st-4th grade	Pancho Rabbit and the Coyote: A Migrant's Tale	Duncan Tonatiuh

Grade 5 Sample Reading Lists

Topic: Building Blocks

Essential Question: How different can two things be if they're made from the same ingredients?

TEXT COMPLEXITY	BOOK TITLE	AUTHOR
5th-7th grade	The Periodic Table: Elements with Style!	Simon Basher and Adrian Dingle
4th-8th grade	Empire State Building	Elizabeth Mann
2nd-6th grade	Esquivel!: Space-Age Sound Artist	Susan Wood
4th-8th grade	Monet and the Impressionists for Kids: Their Lives and Ideas, 21 Activities	Carol Sabbath
3rd-6th grade	Fanny in France: Travel Adventures of a Chef's Daughter, with Recipes	Alice Waters
5th-8th grade	A Wind in the Door	Madeleine L'Engle
4th-7th grade	Miss Ellicott's School for the Magically Minded	Sage Blackwood
3rd-7th grade	Lostman's River	Cynthia DeFelice
4th-6th grade	Project Mulberry	Linda Sue Park
2nd-5th grade	Jake Drake, Know-It-All	Andrew Clements

Topic: Roles and Responsibilities

Essential Question: How important is fairness in dividing up work that needs to be done?

TEXT COMPLEXITY	BOOK TITLE	AUTHOR
4th-6th grade	The Sweetest Sound	Sherrie Winston
3rd-5th grade	Mighty Jack	Ben Hatke
5th-8th grade	The Great Greene Heist	Varian Johnson
5th-8th grade	Patina	Jason Reynolds
4th-8th grade	Children of the Longhouse	Joseph Bruchac
3rd-7th grade	John Lewis in the Lead: A Story of the Civil Rights Movement	Jim Haskins and Benny Andrews
3rd-5th grade	The Life and Times of the Honeybee	Charles Micucci
1st-5th grade	Nurse, Soldier, Spy: The Story of Sarah Edmonds, a Civil War Hero	Marissa Moss
2nd-5th grade	Ada's Violin: The Story of the Recycled Orchestra of Paraguay	Susan Hood
5th-8th grade	Stubby the War Dog: The True Story of World War I's Bravest Dog	Ann Bausum

ENGAGING™ LEARNERS

Grade 5 Sample Reading Lists

Topic: Democracy

Essential Question: Why should we value democracy?

TEXT COMPLEXITY	BOOK TITLE	AUTHOR
5th-7th grade	Johnny Tremain	Esther Forbes
5th-9th grade	The Firefly Letters: A Suffragette's Journey to Cuba	Margarita Engle
3rd-7th grade	Glory Be	Augusta Scattergood
3rd-7th grade	The Kid Who Ran For President	Dan Gutman
3rd-7th grade	The Great Little Madison	Jean Fritz
4th-7th grade	Vote!: The Complicated Life of Claudia Cristina Cortez	Diana Gallagher
4th-8th grade	Lives of the Presidents: Fame, Shame (and What the Neighbors Thought)	Kathleen Krull
3rd-5th grade	Suffrage Sisters: The Fight for Liberty	Maggie Mead
3rd-5th grade	The Ancient Greeks (Spotlights)	Charles Freeman

Topic: Making Predictions

Essential Question: What causes us to be timid, confident, or overconfident, and how can we aim for the right one?

TEXT COMPLEXITY	BOOK TITLE	AUTHOR
2nd-5th grade	The Lemonade War	Jacqueline Davies
4th-8th grade	Last Day on Mars	Kevin Emerson
3rd-6th grade	Harry Potter and the Prisoner of Azkaban	J.K. Rowling
5th-8th grade	The Celebrated Jumping Frog of Calaveras County	Mark Twain
4th-6th grade	The Evolution of Calpurnia Tate	Jacqueline Kelly
5th-7th grade	Do You Wanna Bet?: Your Chance to Find Out About Probability	Jean Cushman
5th-9th grade	How to Lie with Statistics	Darrell Huff
3rd-6th grade	In the Next Three Seconds	Rowland Morgan
5th-7th grade	When the Sky Breaks: Hurricanes, Tornadoes, and the Worst Weather in the World	Simon WInchester
3rd-6th grade	If: A Mind-Bending New Way of Looking at Big Ideas and Numbers	David J. Smith

Grade 5 Sample Reading Lists

Topic: Friendship

Essential Question: What do we have the right to expect from our friends?

TEXT COMPLEXITY	BOOK TITLE	AUTHOR
4th-7th grade	Sputnik's Guide to Life on Earth	Frank Cottrell-Boyce
3rd-7th grade	You Go First	Erin Entrada Kelly
3rd-6th grade	Flora & Ulysses	Kate DiCamillo
5th-8th grade	The Thing About Jellyfish	Ali Benjamin
4th-6th grade	Otherwise Known as Sheila the Great	Judy Blume
5th-6th grade	Navigating Early	Clare Vanderpool
3rd-5th grade	Those Rebels, John and Tom	Barbara Kerley
4th-7th grade	Real Friends	Shannon Hale
5th-8th grade	The Case of the Missing Moonstone	Jordan Stratford

ENGAGING™
LEARNERS

Grade 5 Sample Reading Lists

Topic: Courage

Essential Question: How can a brave person inspire others to be brave as well?

TEXT COMPLEXITY	BOOK TITLE	AUTHOR
5th-8th grade	The Wonder of Charlie Anne	Kimberly Newton Fusco
5th-7th grade	Out of Bounds: Seven Stories of Conflict and Hope	Beverley Naidoo
6th-8th grade	The Boy Who Dared	Susan Campbell Bartoletti
5th-7th grade	All Rise for the Honorable Perry T. Cook	Leslie Connor
5th-7th grade	Number the Stars	Lois Lowry
5th-7th grade	Breaker Boys: How a Photograph Helped End Child Labor	Michael Burgan
6th-9th grade	The Port Chicago 50: Disaster, Mutiny, and the Fight for Civil Rights	Steve Sheinkin
3rd-7th grade	Ugly	Robert Hoge
6th-9th grade	Game Changers: The Unsung Heroines of Sports History	Molly Schiot
3rd-7th grade	Who Is Malala Yousafzai?	Dinah Brown

Topic: Ancient Civilizations

Essential Question: In what ways are our lives alike to those who lived thousands of years ago?

TEXT COMPLEXITY	BOOK TITLE	AUTHOR
4th-8th grade	Cleopatra VII: Daughter of the Nile, Egypt, 57 B.C.	Kristiana Gregory
4th-6th grade	Voyage with Jason	Ken Catran
6th-8th grade	The Eagle of the Ninth	Rosemary Sutcliff
5th-7th grade	The Iron Ring	Lloyd Alexander
6th-9th grade	The Kite Rider	Geraldine McCaughrean
6th-8th grade	Your Travel Guide to Ancient Mayan Civilization	Nancy Raines Day
5th-8th grade	Mansa Musa and the Empire of Mali	P. James Oliver
5th-7th grade	City: A Story of Roman Planning and Construction	David Macaulay
6th-8th grade	Ancient Mesopotamia: The Sumerians, Babylonians, and Assyrians	Virginia Schomp
4th-7th grade	The Story of Ancient China	Suzanne Strauss

Grade 6 Sample Reading Lists

Topic: Earth's Moon

Essential Question: How would our planet be different without the presence of the Moon?

TEXT COMPLEXITY	BOOK TITLE	AUTHOR
4th-7th grade	I Love You, Michael Collins	Lauren Baratz-Logsted
3rd-7th grade	Space Case	Stuart Gibbs
3rd-6th grade	Doctor Dolittle in the Moon	Hugh Lofting
6th-10th grade	From the Earth to the Moon	Jules Verne
3rd-7th grade	The Wonderful Flight to the Mushroom Planet	Eleanor Cameron
6th-9th grade	The Space Race: How the Cold War Put Humans on the Moon	Matthew Brendan Wood
6th-8th grade	A Look At Moons	Kit Moser and Ray Spangenburg
5th-7th grade	Man on the Moon	Pamela Dell
5th-8th grade	When The Sun Goes Dark	Andrew Fraknoi and Dennis Schatz
4th-6th grade	Who Was Galileo?	Patricia Brennan Demuth

Topic: Change

Essential Question: How can we judge whether change is happening too quickly, too slowly, or just right?

TEXT COMPLEXITY	BOOK TITLE	AUTHOR
5th-8th grade	Feathers	Jacqueline Woodson
3rd-7th grade	Counting on Grace	Elizabeth Winthrop
6th-9th grade	5 to 1	Holly Bodger
4th-7th grade	Jump Back Paul: The Life & Poems of Paul Laurence Dunbar	Sally Derby and Paul Laurence Dunbar
3rd-7th grade	Honeybee	Naomi Shihab Nye
3rd-6th grade	Minds-On Matter: Phase Changes And Physical Properties	Jessica Fries-Gaither and Terry Shiverdecker
6th-10th grade	What If?: Serious Scientific Answers to Absurd Hypothetical Questions	Randall Munroe
5th-8th grade	Finding Wonders: Three Girls Who Changed Science	Jeannine Atkins
5th-8th grade	Why'd They Wear That?: Fashion as the Mirror of History	Sarah Albee

Grade 6 Sample Reading Lists

Topic: Dreaming Big

Essential Question: What habits help turn ambitions into reality?

TEXT COMPLEXITY	BOOK TITLE	AUTHOR
3rd-7th grade	Katerina's Wish	Jeannie Mobley
4th-7th grade	Olivia Bean, Trivia Queen	Donna Gephart
3rd-6th grade	Landed	Milly Lee
6th-10th grade	The Crossover	Kwame Alexander
4th-6th grade	El Lector	William Durbin
3rd-6th grade	Zita the Spacegirl	Ben Hatke
5th-7th grade	The Same Stuff as Stars	Katherine Paterson
3rd-7th grade	Hidden Figures: Young Readers' Edition	Margot Lee Shetterly
5th-8th grade	How to Be a Math Genius	Mike Goldsmith

Grade 7 Sample Reading Lists

Topic: Rebellion

Essential Question: What actions or inactions make it necessary to defy authority?

TEXT COMPLEXITY	BOOK TITLE	AUTHOR
4th-7th grade	Breaking Stalin's Nose	Eugene Yelchin
6th-9th grade	Of Fire and Stars	Audrey Coulthurst
5th-9th grade	Chains	Laurie Halse Anderson
6th-12th grade	Divergent	Veronica Roth
5th-7th grade	The Great Gilly Hopkins	Katherine Paterson
7th-10th grade	Scorpions	Walter Dean Myers
7th-10th grade	Saints	Gene Luen Yang
6th-8th grade	The American Revolutionaries: A History in Their Own Words 1750-1800	Milton Meltzer
5th-7th grade	Abraham Lincoln Vs. Jefferson Davis: Presidents of a Divided Nation	Ellis Roxburgh
7th-11th grade	Speak a Word for Freedom: Women Against Slavery	Janet Willen and Marjorie Gann

Topic: Synergy

Essential Question: What are ways to balance contributing to a greater good with following your own dreams?

TEXT COMPLEXITY	BOOK TITLE	AUTHOR
5th-8th grade	Ninth Ward	Jewell Parker Rhodes
3rd-7th grade	MiNRS	Kevin Sylvester
3rd-7th grade	Pablo and Birdy	Alison McGhee
4th-8th grade	Garvey's Choice	Nikki Grimes
7th-10th grade	Vandal	Michael Simmons
3rd-7th grade	Tree of Life: The Incredible Biodiversity of Life on Earth	Rochelle Strauss
7th-12th grade	The World Without Us	Alan Weisman
6th-9th grade	A Closer Look at Biology, Microbiology, and the Cell	Sherman Hollar
4th-7th grade	Swamper: Letters from a Louisiana Swamp Rabbit	Amy Griffin Ouchley

ENGAGING™
LEARNERS

Grade 7 Sample Reading Lists

Topic: Adaption

Essential Question: How much can someone change without losing their previous identity?

TEXT COMPLEXITY	BOOK TITLE	AUTHOR
4th-7th grade	The Higher Power of Lucky	Susan Patron
5th-8th grade	Tunnel Through Time	Lester del Rey
7th-10th grade	Soulprint	Megan Miranda
6th-9th grade	Then Again, Maybe I Won't	Judy Blume
5th-8th grade	The Shakespeare Stealer	Gary L. Blackwood
5th-7th grade	Stronger Than Steel: Spider Silk DNA and the Quest for Better Bulletproof Vests, Sutures, and Parachute Rope	Bridget Heos
7th-11th grade	March onto Land: The Silurian Period to the Middle Triassic Epoch	Thom Holmes
6th-10th grade	The Mesozoic Era: Age of Dinosaurs	John P. Rafferty
7th-11th grade	Biodiversity	Natalie Goldstein
6th-10th grade	Natural Attraction: A Field Guide to Friends, Frenemies, and Other Symbiotic Animal Relationships	Iris Gottlieb

Topic: Migrations

Essential Question: What do people mean when they call a place home?

TEXT COMPLEXITY	BOOK TITLE	AUTHOR
6th-9th grade	The Hired Girl	Laura Amy Schlitz
3rd-7th grade	Tonight, By Sea	Frances Temple
5th-7th grade	The Road to Memphis	Mildred D. Taylor
7th-10th grade	Starglass	Phoebe North
6th-8th grade	Enrique's Journey	Sonia Nazario
3rd-8th grade	The Great Migration: Journey to the North	Eloise Greenfield
6th-8th grade	It Ain't So Awful, Falafel	Firoozeh Dumas
3rd-7th grade	On the Wing: American Birds in Migration	Carol Lerner
7th-9th grade	Otzi the Iceman	Amanda Lanser
5th-8th grade	Chernobyl's Wild Kingdom: Life in the Dead Zone	Rebecca L. Johnson

Grade 7 Sample Reading Lists

Topic: Familial Relationships

Essential Question: To what extent is family part of a person's destiny, and to what is extent is family chosen?

TEXT COMPLEXITY	BOOK TITLE	AUTHOR
5th-8th grade	Crow	Barbara Wright
5th-7th grade	The Westing Game	Ellen Raskin
4th-7th grade	Welcome to Nowhere	Elizabeth Laird
7th-11th grade	This Side of Home	Renee Watson
4th-8th grade	Gone Crazy in Alabama	Rita Williams-Garcia
7th-11th grade	Breaking Night	Liz Murray
7th-10th grade	Samurai Rising: The Epic Life of Minamoto Yoshitsune	Pamela S. Turner
6th-9th grade	See You at Harry's	Jo Knowles
6th-10th grade	Genetics: Breaking the Code of Your DNA	Carla Mooney
7th-10th grade	I Am Not Your Perfect Mexican Daughter	Erika L. Sanchez

**ENGAGING™
LEARNERS**

Grade 8 Sample Reading Lists

Topic: Revision

Essential Question: What does it mean to say a thing is finished?

TEXT COMPLEXITY	BOOK TITLE	AUTHOR
4th-8th grade	11 Birthdays	Wendy Mass
7th-10th grade	The Count of Monte Cristo	Alexandre Dumas
4th-8th grade	Timmy Failure: Mistakes Were Made	Stephan Pastis
8th-12th grade	Lab Girl	Hope Jahren
7th-9th grade	The Story of Science: Aristotle Leads the Way	Joy Hakim
7th-10th grade	Chien-Shiung Wu: Nuclear Physicist	Nel Yomtov
6th-9th grade	A Kids' Guide to America's Bill of Rights: Curfews, Censorship, and the 100-Pound Giant	Kathleen Krull
3rd-8th grade	A Pebble for Your Pocket	Thich Nhat Hanh
8th-12th grade	The Elements of Style	William Strunk and E.B. White
6th-9th grade	The Longitude Prize	Joan Dash

Topic: Misfortune

Essential Question: To what extent do we control our own destinies?

TEXT COMPLEXITY	BOOK TITLE	AUTHOR
7th-10th grade	Tyrell	Coe Booth
5th-9th grade	Zane and the Hurricane	Rodman Philbrick
4th-8th grade	War Horse	Michael Morpurgo
5th-8th grade	Bodies from the Ash: Life and Death in Ancient Pompeii	James M. Deem
8th-10th grade	A Time of Troubles	Pieter Van Raven
8th-11th grade	Behind the Beautiful Forevers: Life, Death and Hope in a Mumbai Undercity	Katherine Boo
8th-11th grade	Me and Earl and the Dying Girl	Jesse Andrews
8th-10th grade	The Family Romanov	Candace Fleming
5th-8th grade	The San Francisco Earthquake of 1906	Marcia Amidon Lusted
7th-12th grade	A Grief Observed	C.S. Lewis

Grade 8 Sample Reading Lists

Topic: Settling the Earth

Essential Question: How does our relationship with the land we inhabit and/or own define us as people?

TEXT COMPLEXITY	BOOK TITLE	AUTHOR
7th-10th grade	The Rest of Us Just Live Here	Patrick Ness
8th-11th grade	Run, Riot	Nikesh Shukla
8th-11th grade	Out of the Blue	Sophie Cameron
7th-9th grade	The Distance Between Lost and Found	Kathryn Holmes
8th-11th grade	A History of the World in 6 Glasses	Tom Standage
7th-9th grade	Simón Bolívar: Fighting for Latin American Liberation	Barbara C. Cruz
7th-10th grade	The Boy Who Harnessed the Wind	William Kamkwamba
7th-9th grade	Up to This Pointe	Jennifer Longo
7th-10th grade	John Winthrop, Oliver Cromwell, and the Land of Promise	Marc Aronson

Topic: Exponential Growth/Decay

Essential Question: How quickly must we react to the different challenges that face us?

TEXT COMPLEXITY	BOOK TITLE	AUTHOR
7th-10th grade	Need	Joelle Charbonneau
8th-11th grade	I am Waltz	Matthew D. Dho
4th-8th grade	Frank Einstein and the Antimatter Motor	Jon Scieszka
8th-11th grade	Expiration Day	William Campbell Powell
6th-10th grade	Seven Billion and Counting: The Crisis in Global Population Growth	Michael M. Andregg
7th-9th grade	Grace Hopper: Computer Scientist	Jill C. Wheeler
7th-10th grade	Pure Grit: How American World War II Nurses Survived Battle and Prison Camp in the Pacific	Mary Cronk Farrell
8th-11th grade	Life by the Numbers	Keith Devlin
5th-8th grade	Outbreak: Plagues that Changed History	Bryn Barnard

ENGAGING™
LEARNERS

Grade 8 Sample Reading Lists

Topic: Communication Networks

Essential Question: How do the ways in which we talk to people change the kinds of conversations we have?

TEXT COMPLEXITY	BOOK TITLE	AUTHOR
8th-10th grade	Eliza and her Monster	Francesca Zappia
7th-9th grade	The Future of Us	Jay Asher and Carolyn Mackler
7th-12th grade	I'll Give You The Sun	Jandy Nelson
8th-10th grade	Free to Fall	Lauren Miller
8th-12th grade	Circumference: Eratosthenes and the Ancient Quest to Measure the Globe	Nicholas Nicastro
7th-10th grade	Rumors of Peace	Ella Leffland
6th-9th grade	Riders of the Pony Express	Ralph Moody
8th-12th grade	Writing on the Wall: Social Media - The First 2,000 Years	Tom Standage
8th-10th grade	Replay: The History of Video Games	Tristan Donovan

Grade 8 Sample Reading Lists

Topic: Scarcity

Essential Question: When is it alright to use something that you cannot replenish?

TEXT COMPLEXITY	BOOK TITLE	AUTHOR
8th-11th grade	Powering Forward: What Everyone Should Know About America's Energy Revolution	Bill Ritter, Jr.
10th-12th grade	How to Cool the Planet: Geoengineering and the Audacious Quest to Fix Earth's Climate	Jeff Goodell
5th-9th grade	World Without Fish	Mark Kurlansky
6th-10th grade	Black Potatoes: The Story of the Great Irish Famine, 1845-1850	Susan Campbell Bartoletti
10th-12th grade	Everybody Loves a Good Drought	P. Sainath
9th-11th grade	Memory of Water	Emmi Itaranta
9th-12th grade	Foundation	Isaac Asimov
8th-10th grade	The Pearl	John Steinbeck
5th-9th grade	The Midwife's Apprentice	Karen Cushman
6th-10th grade	Being Fishkill	Ruth Lehrer

Topic: Sacrifice

Essential Question: How do self-interest and selflessness both play a role in making a sacrifice?

TEXT COMPLEXITY	BOOK TITLE	AUTHOR
7th-9th grade	Churchill and the Battle of Britain: Days of Decision	Nicola Barber
10th-12th grade	Long Walk to Freedom: The Autobiography of Nelson Mandela	Nelson Mandela
9th-12th grade	The Selfish Gene	Richard Dawkins
9th-12th grade	Beyond Words: What Animals Think and Feel	Carl Safina
7th-10th grade	The Champions' Game	Saul Ramirez
8th-12th grade	A Tale of Two Cities	Charles Dickens
8th-10th grade	The Lottery and Other Stories	Shirley Jackson
7th-10th grade	The Rock and the River	Kekla Magoon
9th-12th grade	The Distance Between Us	Reyna Grande
7th-9th grade	Uprising	Margaret Peterson Haddix

ENGAGING LEARNERS

Grades 9/10 Sample Reading Lists

Topic: Fame

Essential Question: What extra responsibilities do prominent people in society have compared to everyone else?

TEXT COMPLEXITY	BOOK TITLE	AUTHOR
10th-12th grade	Where Am I Now?: True Stories of Girlhood and Accidental Fame	Mara Wilson
9th-11th grade	Hoop Dreams	Ben Joravsky
7th-10th grade	The Borden Murders: Lizzie Borden and the Trial of the Century	Sarah Miller
7th-10th grade	Doping in Sports	Stephanie Sammartino McPherson
9th-12th grade	The Picture of Dorian Gray	Oscar Wilde
10th-12th grade	Eliza and Her Monsters	Francesca Zappia
10th-12th grade	The Beautiful and Damned	F. Scott Fitzgerald
5th-9th grade	Summerlost	Ally Condie
7th-11th grade	Ender's Game	Orson Scott Card
9th-12th grade	Wicked: The Life and Times of the Wicked Witch of the West	Gregory Maguire

Topic: Hope

Essential Question: How does the expectation for a better tomorrow have a real impact on the world?

TEXT COMPLEXITY	BOOK TITLE	AUTHOR
8th-11th grade	Adventures in the Anthropocene: A Journey to the Heart of the Planet We Made	Gaia Vince
7th-9th grade	Breaking Through	Francisco Jimenez
10th-12th grade	The Optimism Bias: A Tour of the Irrationally Positive Brain	Tali Sharot
9th-12th grade	Walden	Henry David Thoreau
7th-9th grade	Fire and Hemlock	Diana Wynne Jones
10th-12th grade	The Lathe of Heaven	Ursula K. Le Guin
10th-12th grade	Abundance: The Future Is Better Than You Think	Peter H. Diamandis
5th-10th grade	The Complete Peanuts Vol. 6: 1961-1962	Charles Schulz
7th-9th grade	A Time to Dance	Padma Venkatraman
8th-10th grade	This is How I Find Her	Sara Polsky

Grades 9/10 Sample Reading Lists

Topic: Enemies

Essential Question: In which ways should we give our antagonists the opportunity to become our friends?

TEXT COMPLEXITY	BOOK TITLE	AUTHOR
10th-12th grade	George, Nicholas and Wilhelm: Three Royal Cousins and the Road to World War I	Miranda Carter
7th-10th grade	Never Cry Wolf	Farley Mowat
10th-12th grade	Lives	Plutarch
6th-10th grade	Tesla vs Edison: The Life-Long Feud that Electrified the World	Nigel Cawthorne
10th-12th grade	Console Wars: Sega, Nintendo, and the Battle that Defined a Generation	Blake J. Harris
10th-12th grade	Burr	Gore Vidal
8th-12th grade	The Final Problem	Arthur Conan Doyle
8th-10th grade	Winning	Lara Deloza
9th-12th grade	Murder on the Orient Express	Agatha Christie
8th-12th grade	Animal Farm	George Orwell

ENGAGING™
LEARNERS

Grades 11/12 Sample Reading Lists

Topic: The Engine and Engineering

Essential Question: What are the limits of efficiency?

TEXT COMPLEXITY	BOOK TITLE	AUTHOR
9th-12th grade	Set Phasers on Stun: And Other True Tales of Design, Technology, and Human Error	S.M. Casey
11th-12th Grade	The Perfectionists: How Precision Engineers Created the Modern World	Simon Winchester
9th-12th grade	Factory Girls	Leslie Chang
11th-12th grade	The Great Bridge: The Epic Story of the Building of the Brooklyn Bridge	David McCullough
9th-11th grade	Geoengineering Earth's Climate: Resetting the Thermostat	Jennifer Swanson
11th-12th grade	Apollo 8: The Thrilling Story of the First Mission to the Moon	Jeffrey Kluger
7th-11th grade	Radioactive!: How Irène Curie and Lise Meitner Revolutionized Science and Changed the World	Winifred Conkling
11th-12th grade	John Henry Days	Colson Whitehead
10th-12th grade	Player Piano	Kurt Vonnegut
9th-12th grade	Binti	Nnedi Okorafor

Topic: Recovery

Essential Question: Does healing from a wound have to involve protecting oneself from suffering the same pain again?

TEXT COMPLEXITY	BOOK TITLE	AUTHOR
11th-12th grade	The Radium Girls: The Dark Story of America's Shining Women	Kate Moore
10th-12th grade	Freedom's Shore	Russell Duncan
8th-12th grade	Laughing at My Nightmare	Shane Burcaw
11th-12th grade	Wave	Sonali Deraniyagala
11th-12th grade	Illness as Metaphor and AIDS and Its Metaphors	Susan Sontag
9th-12th grade	A List of Cages	Robin Roe
10th-11th grade	History Is All You Left Me	Adam Silvera
9th-12th grade	Crank	Ellen Hopkins
11th-12th grade	The Magic Mountain	Thomas Mann
9th-12th grade	I Never Promised You a Rose Garden	Joanne Greenberg

Grades 11/12 Sample Reading Lists

Topic: Finding Reliable Information

Essential Question: When a person sees something they know to be false, what is their responsibility?

TEXT COMPLEXITY	BOOK TITLE	AUTHOR
10th-12th grade	The Brain: The Story of You	David Eagleman
7th-11th grade	A History of Ambition in 50 Hoaxes	Gale Eaton
11th-12th grade	Necessary Illusions: Thought Control in Democratic Societies	Noam Chomsky
11th-12th grade	The History of the Standard Oil Company	Ida M. Tarbell
9th-12th grade	Three Cups of Deceit	Jon Krakauer
9th-12th grade	Never Let Me Go	Kazuo Ishiguro
11th-12th grade	Vanity Fair	William Makepeace Thackeray
10th-12th grade	The Hate U Give	Angie Thomas
11th-12th grade	The God of Small Things	Arundhati Roy
9th-12th grade	The Crucible	Arthur Miller

Topic: Investment

Essential Question: What is the proper balance between planning for the future and enjoying the present?

TEXT COMPLEXITY	BOOK TITLE	AUTHOR
9th-12th grade	Made to Stick: Why Some Ideas Survive and Others Die	Chip Heath and Dan Heath
11th-12th grade	Thinking in Bets: Making Smarter Decisions When You Don't Have All the Facts	Annie Duke
11th-12th grade	The Beekeeper's Lament: How One Man and Half a Billion Honey Bees Help Feed America	Hannah Nordhaus
9th-12th grade	The Triumph of Seeds: How Grains, Nuts, Kernels, Pulses, and Pips Conquered the Plant Kingdom and Shaped Human History	Thor Hanson
11th-12th grade	The Story of the Stone, vol. 1	Cao Xuejin
11th-12th grade	The Mill on the Floss	George Eliot
9th-12th grade	What Makes Sammy Run?	Budd Schulberg
9th-11th grade	Break	Hannah Moskowitz
9th-11th grade	Feed	MT Anderson

Grades 11/12 Sample Reading Lists

Topic: Figures of Speech

Essential Question: How can figurative language sometimes provide more effective communication than literal speech?

TEXT COMPLEXITY	BOOK TITLE	AUTHOR
10th-12th grade	The Collected Poems of William Carlos Williams	William Carlos Williams
10th-12th grade	Poems	Elizabeth Barrett Browning
11th-12th grade	The Masnavi, Book One	Jalal al-Din Rumi
9th-12th grade	The Complete Poems	John Keats
7th-12th grade	Alice's Adventures in Wonderland	Lewis Carroll
10th-12th grade	The Collected Poetry of Nikki Giovanni: 1968-1998	Nikki Giovanni
9th-12th grade	The Pun Also Rises	John Pollack
11th-12th grade	Understanding Media: The Extensions of Man	Marshall McLuhan
11th-12th grade	Known and Strange Things	Teju Cole
9th-12th grade	Mother Tongues	Helena Drysdale

Notes on this Chapter

Chapter 4
Tools for Reading Together Centers

PREP TIME
The first time you do the activity you'll need to write up center directions and prepare an example for the mini-lesson. After that, you'll only need a few minutes to gather materials. Allow 1/2 hour or less.

Sticky Notes
Grades 4–12

Center(s)
Reading Together

Skills
Students practice a close reading strategy while engaging in independent reading. This activity can easily be adapted to encourage students to increase vocabulary by looking for context clues, analyzing texts, or identifying the central and supporting ideas of a text.

Activity Description
This exercise helps students become more active readers by encouraging them to record their thoughts, comments, questions, and personal connections on sticky notes and placing them directly on or by the text that inspired the thought.

Overview
Many fluent readers use the Sticky Note strategy throughout their lives. (Of course if a reader owns the book, they sometimes write directly in the margins!) It's appropriate for fiction and informational text, and can be used in any content-area class as well as for independent reading.

Teacher Tips
When you first introduce the activity, you may want to have students focus on writing one kind of note rather than recording thoughts, comments, questions, and personal connections. Most students find it easy to record questions,

ENGAGING™
LEARNERS

so start with that. Suggest they add a sticky note anytime they don't understand a word or sentence. Then, as they get comfortable with the strategy, suggest they also record comments and thoughts. Finally, recommend that they use sticky notes to record their personal connections to the text.

To encourage students to use this close reading strategy on their own, you may also want to download and display **Poster – Sticky Notes** from the **engaginglearners.com/literacy-learning-centers** resources website

Center Prep
- Text for independent reading (one copy for each student)
- Sticky notes
- Pencils/pens
- Written center instructions

Adjusting the Rigor
After students are comfortable with this activity, you can increase the rigor by asking them to write full sentences on their sticky notes. You can even make this an additional center activity by having groups rework their sentence-fragment notes as a team.

Or pair this with a Speaking & Listening center in which students discuss why readers might have different connections, comments and questions about the same text. How might the knowledge that every reader has different personal connections to a text affect an author?

Mini-Lesson
First, explain the purpose of the Sticky Note strategy by saying something like this:

"Active and independent readers have a voice in their head when reading. Usually this internal voice asks questions, makes comments, or makes a personal connection to the text. As you read your text, use sticky notes to record your questions, comments and personal connections and place them in the corresponding part of your text."

Then model the activity by actively reading a text and adding your own sticky notes. This works well on an overhead projector. For example, imagine I was reading the following paragraph aloud to a 7th grade classroom. I could pause at least 4 or 5 times to write sticky notes. Notice that the notes don't have to be written in complete sentences. In fact, explain to the students that the messages on the sticky notes are just for the reader; they don't have to make sense to anyone else and everyone's will be different.

After annotating the text, read it aloud again without including the sticky note comments. It will help students to hear a fluent reader engage with the text. As they listen and follow along, their inner eyes and inner voices might even see and say some of the same things yours did!

The Star-Spangled Banner:
The Flag that Inspired the National Anthem
from Smithsonian National Museum of American History

On September 14, 1814, U.S. soldiers at Baltimore's [sticky note: Football: Baltimore Ravens! Where is it?] Fort McHenry raised a huge American flag to celebrate a crucial [sticky note: Means important?] victory over British forces during the War of 1812. The sight of those "broad stripes and bright stars" [sticky note: draw a sketch of the American flag] inspired Francis Scott Key to write a song that eventually became the United States national anthem. [sticky note: Song at baseball game] Key's words gave new significance to a national symbol and started a tradition through which generations of Americans have invested the flag with their own meanings and memories. [sticky note: like a photo album]

http://amhistory.si.edu/starspangledbanner/

STICKY NOTES
Sample Center Instructions

Provide written instructions at each center. Your instructions may look something like these samples. Feel free to adapt them to suit your own needs.

DIRECTIONS
Read your book. Use sticky notes to record your questions and comments. We'll discuss these in teacher-led center. Grammar/spelling is **NOT** important as long as you can understand your notes.

READING TOGETHER CENTER DIRECTIONS

1) Choose an essay from the stack.
2) Read your essay independently.
3) Use sticky notes to record comments, questions, or personal connections.

Talking isn't necessary!
Write your comments and questions on a sticky note instead of discussing them with each other.

Remember: These sticky notes record what your internal voice says while you read. They're private - between you and the voice in your head!

You have 10 minutes to read pages 68-70 to yourself. Ask team mates for help if you get stuck.

Write 2-5 thoughts or questions on STICKY NOTES.

The class will work together to turn your sticky notes into complete sentences.

You have permission to reproduce this page for use in your classroom.

ENGAGING™ LEARNERS

STICKY NOTES
Example

Here is an example of the Sticky Note strategy in action:

Such was his state of mind when the Krakatoa sunsets began. The tiny volcanic island of Krakatoa (located halfway between Java and Sumatra) had staged a spectacular eruption at the end of August 1883, jettisoning billions of tonnes of ash and debris deep into the earth's upper atmosphere. Nearly 40,000 people had been killed by a series of mountainous waves thrown out by the force of the explosion: the Javan port of Anjer had been almost completely destroyed, along with more than a hundred coastal towns and villages. "All gone. Plenty lives lost", as a telegram sent from Serang reported, and for weeks afterwards the bodies of the drowned continued to wash up along the shoreline. Meanwhile, the vast volcanic ash-cloud had spread into a semi-opaque band that threaded slowly westward around the equator, forming memorable sunsets and afterglows across the earth's lower latitudes. A few weeks later, the stratospheric veil moved outwards from the tropics to the poles, and by late October 1883 most of the world, including Britain, was being subjected to lurid evening displays, caused by the scattering of incoming light by the meandering volcanic haze. Throughout November and December, the skies flared through virulent shades of green, blue, copper and magenta, "more like inflamed flesh than the lucid reds of ordinary sunsets," wrote Hopkins; "the glow is intense; that is what strikes everyone; it has prolonged the daylight, and optically changed the season; it bathes the whole sky, it is mistaken for the reflection of a great fire."

> **CONNECTION**
> This reminds me of the volcanic eruption a few years ago in Iceland.

> **QUESTION**
> What does "stratospheric" mean?

> **COMMENT**
> It's amazing that a horrible tragedy can create something beautiful too.

The essay is "The Krakatoa Sunsets" from:
https://publicdomainreview.org/2012/05/28/the-krakatoa-sunsets/

PREP TIME
Allow 1-2 hours. At first you might need extra time to find examples of different text structures. As you gain familiarity with the activity, you'll save a lot of time by finding examples during routine reading.

Identifying Text Structures
Grades 4-12

Center(s)
Reading Together

Skills
In this close reading strategy, student readers learn to analyze an informational text to determine its structure – while they are reviewing or learning content. During the discussion step of the activity, students gain experience in citing evidence, conversation, persuasion, and reasoning.

Activity Description
Students read short informational texts to determine which category they fit into: *description, sequence, cause and effect, compare and contrast,* or *problem and solution.*

Center Prep
- A selection of short texts in different categories (print enough so that every group will have a choice)
- Handout: Identifying Text Structures
- Written center instructions
- Timer (optional)

Mini-Lesson
Introduce the activity by reviewing the handout. Explain that even the most intimidating texts often fall into one of these five categories: description, sequence, cause and effect, compare and contrast, or problem and solution.

When a reader is able to identify a text's structure, he or she is more easily able to comprehend its meaning.

After you've explained the purpose of the activity, take a few moments to model it using one or two short texts as examples. Read each text aloud then refer to the handout. Be sure to "think aloud" so that students can clearly see how you decided which structure applies.

For older or more experienced readers, you can explain that complex texts, the kind that readers are likely to encounter in college, sometimes include more than one structure in a single paragraph. For example, you can show a sample text in which an author included sequence as part of a problem and solution structure.

Overview

In the primary grades, most student readers learn to identify common text structures: description, sequence, cause and effect, compare and contrast, or problem and solution.

As they encounter more complicated texts, older readers benefit from ongoing review and development of these skills.

This close reading/comprehension strategy is easily adapted to both ELA and content-area classrooms.

Provide students with a handout describing the five common text structures and a selection of short, content-related texts – these can be excerpted from the textbook or be unfamiliar passages from other sources. Students choose which texts to analyze and then they perform the following two steps for each text that they've chosen.

Step 1
Reading
Teams can choose a team member to read the text aloud or they can read the text silently to themselves.

Step 2
Discussion
Students discuss the structure of the text. During this step, they work toward determining which structure best describes the text. Each reader should be prepared to cite evidence from the text to support his/her claim. (For example, if they determine that the text is and example of a sequence, they should be able to specify the steps to the sequence. If they determine that the text is a description, they should be prepared to identify what person, place, thing or idea is being described.)Then, after listening to everyone's opinion, the group should determine the correct text structure.

Teacher Tips

Students tend to choose shorter texts. So if you want them to concentrate on identifying certain text structures, offer shorter examples of those structures.

You may want to schedule a Teacher-Led center immediately after this Reading Together center. At the Teacher-Led center, give students an opportunity to explain their conclusions and reasoning.

The Identifying Text Structures activity can serve as a great formative assessment tool. You may notice that students are able to identify the style of a text but struggle to cite evidence for their decision. Or they may be confused when a numbered list of traits is included as part of a description, and read it as if it were a list of sequential steps. This gives you the information you need to adjust your lessons and content-review accordingly.

After students are comfortable identifying text structures, you could invite them to brainstorm possible topics that they could write about themselves, using the various text structures.

A good review activity at the end of a unit might include asking students to identify study topics that involve compare/contrast, sequence, description, cause/effect, and problem/solution structures.

Adjusting the Rigor

The activity is an especially valuable way to encourage students to work through texts that might be at the upper limit of their comfort zone.

Advanced student readers might be encouraged to "untangle" readings that include more than one text structure. For example, a single paragraph might begin with a description and conclude with a cause and effect.

Advanced student readers might be provided with texts that are written "out of order." For example, sometimes an author begins a paragraph by describing an effect, and concludes by discussing the cause. Or a paragraph might begin by offering a solution and then describe the problem. Encourage these student readers

to consider why the author may have chosen to organize her/his writing in a less traditional way. Did it create a "mystery" to pique the readers' interest?

Struggling or reluctant student readers might benefit from having fewer options. You could adapt the activity to let them determine if texts are examples of cause and effect or sequence, for example.

IDENTIFYING TEXT STRUCTURES
Sample Center Instructions

There are 6 short texts in the basket. Choose 4 to work on.

1. Pick one member of your group to read your first text aloud. (Help each other if there are difficult words. Remember: YOU ARE A TEAM!)

2. Discuss the text and let everyone say which structure they think it is. Refer to your handout. Be prepared to support your claims.

3. As a group, decide if the text is an example of description, sequence, cause and effect, problem and solution, or compare and contrast.

4. Repeat steps 1-3 until you have analyzed all 4 of your texts. If you have more time, you can analyze another text.

We're going to discuss your work in the Teacher-Led Center when you're done.

IDENTIFYING TEXT STRUCTURES
Sample: Life Science

Here and on the next page are 6 examples of texts used for this activity. They are from a 9th grade life science class that was working on an invasive species unit.

Compare and Contrast

Nonnative constrictors are much longer and heavier than any of Florida's native snakes, routinely growing to more than seven feet long. Their scales appear smooth, unlike the rough, textured scales of native water snakes.

Everglades Cooperative Invasive Species Management Area:
Working to Protect the Everglades from Invasive Species
http://www.evergladescisma.org/the-dirty-dozen/burmese-python/

Cause and Effect

Southern Florida offers a subtropical climate and natural and manmade habitats similar to those found in the tropical regions from which many of the invaders originate. The island-like geography of Florida's southern peninsula and the fact that the region is isolated from areas of similar climate mean that there are relatively few native species to compete with the invaders, allowing them to thrive and spread.

Florida: An Invasive Species Hotspot
http://edis.ifas.ufl.edu/uw365

Problem and Solution

Meshaka characterized the problem of exotic reptiles and amphibians in Florida as a "runaway train in the making." Prevention of their introduction into the environment is the only guaranteed effective approach to reduce impacts of invasive species.
But for many species the time for prevention is past. To control those that are already established and to prevent further introductions, we need to find sustainable funding for a comprehensive statewide plan that includes the following elements:
1. Screening and Risk Assessment
2. Early Detection and Rapid Response
3. Control and Containment
4. Outreach and Education

The Invasion of Exotic Reptiles and Amphibians in Florida
University of FL Institute of Food and Agricultural Science
http://edis.ifas.ufl.edu/pdffiles/UW/UW36500-14inch.pdf

IDENTIFYING TEXT STRUCTURES
Sample Life Science

Sample Texts (Continued)

Description

The Burmese python is a large, nonvenomous constrictor snake that has been introduced to Florida. These snakes represent a threat to the ecosystem, including native wildlife. Burmese pythons can reproduce in great numbers and eat a wide variety of food items ranging from eggs to small deer.

It is believed that Burmese python populations were founded by escaped or released snakes, as early as the 1980s.

Burmese Pythons in Florida: How to Stop the Spread of an
Invasive Snake by Florida Fish and Wildlife Commission
http://myfwc.com/media/2812584/burmesepython.pdf

Sequence

South American floating water hyacinths were introduced into the St. Johns River near Palatka in the late 1880s and soon after made navigation on the river for steamboat traffic almost impossible. Later, a 1950s plant invader, hydrilla (a native of Southeast Asia), began to infest and degrade Florida's lakes and rivers when it produced dense canopies at the surface. Beginning in the 1960s, the Australian melaleuca tree and the South American Brazilian pepper tree began to rapidly spread into and on south Florida's conservation lands.

Invasive Plant Management | Florida Fish
and Wildlife Conservation Commission
http://myfwc.com/wildlifehabitats/invasive-plants/

Compare and Contrast

Cane toads are native to South and Central America and have become established in central and southern Florida. The poison glands on the shoulders of cane toads produce toxins that can kill pets or make them very ill. Native southern toads and oak toads also have these glands, but their toxins are much less potent and are harmless to pets. Native southern toads and invasive cane toads both lay long strings of eggs, and it is nearly impossible to tell their eggs and young apart.

Florida Invader: Cane Toad
By Steve A. Johnson and Monica E. McGarrity |
University of Florida IFAS Extension

ENGAGING™
LEARNERS

IDENTIFYING TEXT STRUCTURES
Handout

Structure	Description	Clue words and phrases		Example
DESCRIPTION	The text describes a person, place, thing or idea by listing its features, or characteristics, or by providing examples. The purpose is usually to help the reader understand how something looks, sounds, feels, tastes, smells or seems.	Similies: looks like sounds like feels like tastes like smells like Consists of Includes For instance	Adjectives: colors sizes textures sounds flavors Characteristics of Such as For example	Oil paint has been used for centuries. It consists of pigment mixed with drying oils. The characteristics of a good quarterback include a strong throwing arm, team leadership, and good reading skills.
SEQUENCE	The text lists steps in a procedure or events in chronological order. The purpose is to describe the order of events or explain how to do something.	Next Then After Following On (date) At (time)	First, second, third... While During Eventually In the end Finally	First crack the egg into the bowl then beat it with a fork. Weathering breaks down rock into tiny pieces called sediment. Then, after many years, wind and water move the sediment far from its original source.
CAUSE AND EFFECT	The text describes an event (a cause) and the effects that follow. The purpose is to explain why or how something happened.	Because If...then So Since Caused by Result Thus	Outcome Brought about by Leads to Therefore Effects of Reasons why Means that	Doug had a good check up last month because he brushed his teeth twice a day. Molecules move quickly when the water is heated, thus causing the water to boil.
COMPARE AND CONTRAST	The text talks about similarities and differences between two or more people, places or things. The purpose is to describe how things are similar or how they are different.	Both All/none Either...or Differs from Similar to In contrast	Neither As well as On the other hand Instead of However Same as	The battle at Shiloh and the battle at Gettysburg were both Union victories, but there were far more casualties at Gettysburg. Carrots have more vitamins, however cake is tastier.
PROBLEM AND SOLUTION	The text describes a problem and offers one or more possible solutions. The purpose is to offer a solution or to describe how others have solved a problem.	Problem Challenge Difficulty Dilemma Puzzle Question	Solution Solve Resolve Answer to If...then Tried/try	The cat had difficulty swallowing pills so Olga mixed the medication into his food. If your ice cream melts too quickly, try standing in the shade.

You have permission to reproduce this page for use in your classroom.

© 2019 Engaging Learners, LLC

PREP TIME

It usually takes 1/2 to 1 hour to find a compound or complex sentence and draft simple sentences. The first time you do the activity you'll need to write up center directions and prepare an example for the mini-lesson.

Break It Up

Grades 4-12

Center(s)

Reading Together

Skills

Practice isolating ideas in a compound or complex sentence while reviewing content. Gain experience in textual analysis, exploring text structure, and considering the author's word choice, style choice, and grammar.

Overview

Complex and compound sentences often intimidate struggling and reluctant readers. Give students an opportunity to practice "breaking up" a long sentence into multiple short sentences that make it easier to understand the author's meaning.

This close reading/comprehension strategy is easily adapted to both ELA and content-area classrooms. It can be used alone at the Reading Together center, or in tandem with the BREAK IT UP YOURSELF activity at the Writer's Craft Center (see Chapter 6).

Teacher Tips

If you're unsure how to create simple sentences out of a complex sentence, let the punctuation tip you off. Commas, semicolons, dashes, and parentheses – as well as "connecting words" like *and* and *but* – are hints that a long sentence could be broken up into little sentences! For more

information about compound and complex sentences, visit this helpful website: **quickanddirtytips.com/grammar-girl**. (Mignon Fogarty is Grammar Girl. Her easy to understand explanations make sense to people who aren't English teachers.)

Mini-Lesson

Model the activity by "breaking up" a complex or compound sentence into short, simple sentences. Remind students that punctuation, and conjunctions ("connecting words" like *and*, *but*, and *or*) can serve as clues. They are often used to connect separate thoughts in a complex sentence. Demonstrate that the words in the original complex sentence might have to be rearranged in order to create well-formed simple sentences.

Center Prep

- A compound/complex sentence related to your content or from your current reading, typed or written out
- Simple sentences created from the information in the complex sentence, each one written on a separate index card
- Written center instructions

Activity Description

Step 1
Students read (or attempt to read) the compound/complex sentence together.

Step 2
Students take turns selecting index cards and identifying where each idea expressed in the simple sentences, appears in the complex sentence. They are encouraged to discuss their reasoning with other group members.

Step 3
If time permits, ask students to discuss why an author might want to write a complex sentence instead of many shorter, simple sentences.

Adjusting the Rigor

To make the activity more rigorous, challenge the students to turn over the printed complex sentence so they can't see it. Then, using only the information in the simple sentences (on the index cards), write their own complex sentence.

BREAK IT UP
Sample Center Instructions

AS A GROUP

Read the following complex sentence from one of our optional readings. It includes a lot of information and many ideas!

Take turns choosing index cards – do them one at a time, in any order you want.

INDIVIDUALLY

Read the sentence printed on your index card. It represents one idea from the complex sentence.

Read the complex sentence closely and find the idea represented by your index card sentence.

Hint: The parts of the index card sentence (subject, verb, object) might not be "all in a row" in the complex sentence. And sometimes the ideas are implied rather than stated, so you might have to really look hard!

Repeat until you're done with all the index cards.

IF YOU HAVE TIME

Discuss – Why do you think the author chose to write one complex sentence instead of many shorter sentences?

BREAK IT UP
Example: Science

COMPLEX SENTENCE TAKEN FROM A SUPPLEMENTAL READING:

> **Discovery: Turn your eyes to the skies for the latest explorers**
> *By Aaron Dubrow, National Science Foundation, August 18, 2016*
>
> "From strengthening wildlife conservation efforts to improving disaster response, researchers are finding new ways to use small, unmanned aerial vehicles (UAVs) -- also known as drones or unmanned aerial systems (UAS) -- to gather data, improve communication, and explore environments where humans and larger aircraft dare not go."
>
> https://www.nsf.gov/discoveries/disc_summ.jsp?cntn_id=189521&org=NSF&from=news

SIMPLE SENTENCES WRITTEN ON INDEX CARDS:

Researchers are finding new ways to use small, unmanne aerial vehicles.

Researchers are finding new ways to use drones to improve communication.

Researchers are finding new ways to use drones to gather data.

Researchers are finding new ways to use drones to strengthen wildlife conservation efforts.

UAS is an abbreviation for "unmanned aerial system".

UAV is an abbreviation for "unmanned aerial vehicle".

Unmanned aerial vehicle is another term for "drone".

Researchers are finding new ways to use drones to explore environments where humans and larger aircraft dare not go.

Researchers are finding new ways to use drones to improve disaster response.

ENGAGING™ LEARNERS

BREAK IT UP
Example: History

COMPLEX SENTENCE TAKEN FROM A SUPPLEMENTAL READING:

Encyclopedia Britannica Article: World War I
Written by: John Graham Royde-Smith

"World War I was one of the great watersheds of 20th-century geopolitical history; it led to the fall of four great imperial dynasties (in Germany, Russia, Austria-Hungary, and Turkey), resulted in the Bolshevik Revolution in Russia, and, in its destabilization of European society, laid the groundwork for World War II.

https://www.britannica.com/event/World-War-I

SIMPLE SENTENCES WRITTEN ON INDEX CARDS:

World War I was one of the great watersheds of 20th-century geopolitical history.

Destabilization of European society laid the groundwork for World War II.

World War I resulted in the Bolshevik Revolution in Russia.

World War I laid the groundwork for World War II.

There were imperial dynasties in Germany, Russia, Austria-Hungary, and Turkey.

World War I resulted in destabilization of European society.

World War I led to the fall of four great imperial dynasties.

This activity requires very little advance preparation. It usually takes 1/2 hour or less to write center instructions and organize your thoughts to prepare for the mini-lesson.

Write a Quiz

Grades 4-12

Center(s)
Reading Together
Writer's Craft

Skills
Students gain practice in textual analysis, reasoning, details, routine writing, revising and editing.

Overview
This activity is perfect for a review, after a text has been read by the entire class (either as a group or independently). Ask students, "If you were the teacher, and you wanted to make sure people really understood this material, what questions would you ask?" Let students determine the most important elements of a text and have them write three short-answer questions for the quiz. Encourage teams to revise their questions so that they are as clear and succinct as possible.

Center Prep
- Writing materials (paper, pencils, etc.)
- A copy of the text
- Written center instructions

ENGAGING LEARNERS

Mini-Lesson

Review elements of what makes a good short-answer test question:

- It should be clear.
- It shouldn't have more than one possible answer.
- It should be about important material that was covered in the text.

Review tips for determining the most important elements of a text:

- Check headlines and bold words/phrases.
- Analyze the meaning of illustrations and graphics.

Teacher Tips

Review the students' questions and then actually use them in a quiz! Of course you may need to revise them for clarity. You can add your own questions to the mix, especially if you get a lot of duplication from your teams or if students overlooked something that you feel is important. Students love writing their own quizzes and don't even realize that they're reviewing content.

If you're attempting to review an entire chapter, students will tend to write questions only on the early pages. Assign groups different sections so that the all the content is covered.

WRITE A QUIZ
Sample Center Instructions

Provide written instructions at the center. Your instructions may look something like this sample. Feel free to adapt this to suit your classroom's needs.

1. As a team, write three short-answer questions for tomorrow's quiz on Section 2, Westward Bound.

    - What is some of the most important information your classmates should understand about travel before the Civil War?

2. Pass your questions around the group for revisions. Review and proofread them carefully.

    - Can each question be answered with one sentence or phrase?

    - Is everything spelled correctly?

    - Is the question easy to understand?

Snapchat the Main Point
Grades 4-12

Center(s)
This multi-center activity incorporates the following centers:
Reading Together
Speaking & Listening
Writer's Craft
Teacher-Led

Skills
Students work together on reading goals (identifying a central idea, summarization, citing evidence), speaking & listening goals (conversation, reasoning, citing evidence, presenting information), and writing goals (task/purpose/audience, production, planning, revising and editing).

Overview
This engaging activity is a great replacement for those boring quizzes or "paraphrase" exercises that we sometimes fall back on. It can be used with any content area text.

Students start this activity in the Reading Together center. Then they move to a Speaking & Listening Center for planning. Finally, they move to a Writer's Craft center to write a Snapchat summarization. The teacher can assess the students' work and provide support at any step along the way.

The activity concludes with students sharing their pretend Snapchats with the class. You're bound to see some entertaining pictures and funny sentences. But when you assess for understanding, look for messages that truly encapsulate the author's topic sentence or main idea. While Snapchat messages can be quite short, give extra applause to students who use exactly 80 characters. And scan the sketches for details. The drawings don't have to be well executed (not everyone is an artist!) but they should include specificity to indicate that the students examined the text closely and were able to make inferences from what they read.

Teacher Tip

Students can count out their characters manually or they can use a word processing program or an online character counter like **www.lettercount.com**.

Center Prep

- A selection of short, content-related texts
- Writing materials, paper and pencils
- Timer (optional)
- Written center instructions

Activity Description

After reading a text together, students summarize the author's main point using nothing but a quick sketch and 80 or fewer characters.

Adjusting the Rigor

Ask students to use exactly 80 characters. This will require them to revise their grammar, use of punctuation, and word choice. You may want to allow them to use a thesaurus or personal dictionary if necessary. And if your school's technology plan permits, students can use real Snapchat to create and share their summaries of the author's main point! They can include staged photos instead of drawings. In this variation of the activity, students would also be working toward the goals of technology, media, and publishing.

Mini-Lesson

Review the concept of summarization with the students before beginning the activity. Remind them that authors sometimes include their own summarization in their topic sentence and/or concluding sentence, but other times it takes a strong reader to be able to identify an author's main point and construct a summary. Model summarization using examples of both kinds of texts.

This is also a good time to review that, for the purposes of this activity, a Snapchat is a picture with a brief caption (80 characters or less). It's meant to be viewed quickly because it will self-destruct within a few seconds. Show examples of student samples if possible.

A student sample of a completed Snapchat the Main Point activity follows on the next page.

Notes

_____

_____

_____

_____

_____

_____

_____

_____

_____

_____

SNAPCHAT THE MAIN POINT
Example

To finish our discussion of fantasy animals, choose one of the
bookmarked articles about mermaids, dragons, or jackalopes :

How Did Manatees Inspire Mermaid Legends? from National Geographic News
Where Did Dragons Come From? from Smithsonian.com
The World's Scariest Rabbit Lurks Within the Smithsonian's Collection from Smithsonian Insider

Snapchat the Main Point

Names *Marri Louis Trent*

The name of the article we read: <u>THE WORLD'S SCARIEST RABBIT LURKS</u>
— <u>WITHIN THE SMITHSONIAN'S COLLECTION</u>

Our picture:

Our caption (80 characters or less – try to get exactly 80!)

<u>Jackalopes can be real, but the rabbit's antlers are,</u>

<u>because of a papilloma virus</u>

ENGAGING™
LEARNERS

SNAPCHAT THE MAIN POINT
Sample Center Instructions

Provide written instructions at each center. Your instructions may look something like these samples. Feel free to adapt them to suit your own needs.

Reading Together Center

Set the timer for 1 minute:
Choose one of the three short texts to read together.

Set the timer for 9 minutes:
Read the chosen text together as a group. Look up any unfamiliar words.
Help each other and make sure that everyone understands the text.

Speaking & Listening Center

Set the timer for 5 minutes:
Discuss the author's main point. If you disagree with each other remember to support your opinions by citing evidence from the text.

Set the timer for 5 minutes:
Decide as a group what 1-3 things you want to include in your text and picture summarization. Remember, your Snapchat will self-destruct in a few seconds so it has to be simple!

Writer's Craft Center

Set the timer for 1 minute:
Assign jobs.
- The artist(s) – draw the picture
- The writer(s) – write the Snapchat text
- The editor(s) – make sure agreed upon things are included, count the characters, and watch the timer

Set the timer for 6 minutes:
Write, draw, or edit

Set the timer for 3 minutes:
As a group, review your work, discuss briefly, and revise as necessary.

SNAPCHAT THE MAIN POINT
Sample Timeline

Depending on the length and complexity of the text, you may want to increase the amount of time spent at each center and allow two or three days to complete the activity.

Class is divided up in to 3 groups (X, Y, and Z) of 5 students each.

9:00 - 9:10   Mini-Lesson

9:10 - 9:20   Groups X and Y do Reading Together Center independently;
Group Z does Reading Together activity at a Teacher-Led Center.

9:20 - 9:30   Groups Z and X do Speaking & Listening Center independently;
Group Y does Speaking & Listening activity at a Teacher-Led Center.

9:30 -9:40   Groups Y and Z do Writer's Craft Center independently;
Group X does Writer's Craft activity at a Teacher-Led Center.

9:40 - 9:50   All groups present their Snapchats to the full class

9:50 - 10:00   Reflection and full class discussion

ENGAGING™ LEARNERS

We can help you build student achievement

The Engaging Learners team can come to YOU!

Sometimes modeling is the best way to help teachers see the power of Literacy & Learning Centers. We work with school leadership to create customized professional development that addressed each school's unique challenges— including hands on work in your classrooms. We can help you prepare your students for amazing literacy growth. Visit **www.EngagingLearners.com/on-site** for more info.

Notes on this Chapter

Chapter 5
Tools for Vocabulary Centers

PREP TIME
This activity doesn't require much advance preparation. It usually takes about 1/2 hour to write center instructions, prepare for the mini-lesson, and print graphic organizers.

Best Guess Definition
Grades 4–12

Center(s)
Vocabulary

Skills
This graphic organizer activity encourages students to look for context clues, explore what they know about word construction (prefixes, suffixes, and root words) and consider their own prior knowledge, whenever they encounter an unknown word. They conclude the activity by checking their well-reasoned guess with reference materials.

Activity Description
Student readers often need to be reminded that they have a lot of tools at their disposal whenever they encounter an unfamiliar word or phrase. This graphic organizer helps them visualize what they already know about a word (how it's being used in a sentence), and look for clues or hints as to its meaning. They make their own, well-reasoned guess about its definition and then check it against a dictionary definition. This activity is appropriate to help with vocabulary acquisition in any content area.

Overview
Step One
Choose a word or phrase to explore. Let each student choose an unfamiliar word or phrase from their reading that they'd like to explore.

ENGAGING™ LEARNERS

Step Two

Complete a Best Guess Definition graphic organizer for their chosen word or phrase. Ask students to fill in all steps to the best of their ability. There won't always be multiple context clues or prefixes/suffixes/root words – and the part of speech might not be obvious to all students. Students should just fill in whatever information they can and feel free to leave some fields blank if necessary. Conclude by having them check their definition against a reference (dictionary, glossary, textbook, etc.) as indicated.

Step Three

Reflect. Students share their work with other members of the group. They discuss their reasoning and try to imagine how they might be able to use what they learned about this new word the next time they encounter an unfamiliar word or phrase.

Teacher Tips

You can ask students to rotate to a different center for the reflection step of this activity. Or the reflection can be done at a Teacher-Led Center if you feel your students would benefit from a little extra personal attention and support.

This activity is a good follow-up to a close reading activity like Sticky Notes. Ask students to review their comments and choose an unfamiliar word or phrase from their own reading. Alternately, you can do this activity by letting students choose from among new vocabulary words that you provide at the center. If you provide the words, make sure you include them in context. Students will need to see how an unfamiliar word fits into a sentence/paragraph in order to complete the activity.

Center Prep

- Printed copies of Best Guess Definition graphic organizers, one for each student
- Pencils or pens
- A choice of unfamiliar or new words/phrases in context (as part of a text)
- Written center instructions

Mini-Lesson

Start by reminding students that not knowing the exact meaning of a word or phrase is nothing to be embarrassed about. Even the most educated and experienced readers frequently encounter unfamiliar words all the time – that's how they continue to learn new words. Assure students that every time they explore a new word and discover its meaning, they gain more information, resources, and tools for the next time.

Then model the activity by filling out a Best Guess Definition graphic organizer with a new vocabulary word. Be sure to explain your reasoning and include short reviews of concepts (like context clues, parts of speech, etc.) as necessary.

Adjusting the Rigor

Struggling readers might benefit from simplified versions of this graphic organizer. Feel free to create your own versions that focus only on context clues, looking at word construction, or identifying parts of speech. Word processing makes it easy to fashion professional looking graphic organizers, but hand-drawn ones work fine, too!

BEST GUESS DEFINITION

Name:_____

WHAT I KNOW ABOUT THIS WORD

Vocabulary word:

Part of speech:

The text or quote where I first found the word:

MY CLUES

Do I recognize any suffixes, prefixes, or root words?

Does it remind me of other words?

Context clue #1:

Context clue #2:

MY GUESS

My BEST GUESS definition (in my own words):

Last step: check your guess

Use a dictionary or glossary and write the correct definition:

❑ I guessed right (or pretty close!)
❑ I guessed wrong. I'll re-read the passage with the correct definition in mind.

You have permission to reproduce this page for use in your classroom.

 **ENGAGING™ LEARNERS**

BEST GUESS DEFINITION

Best Guess Definition: Example from 5th Grade English Class

Students were using the LLC model to explore support material in preparation for a full-class reading of an edited version of Shakespeare's *Julius Caesar*. During their research, they encountered many new and unfamiliar words/phrases (ides of March, conspiracy, assassination, antiquity, etc.). The teacher created a Vocabulary Center where they could "guess" definitions.

BEST GUESS DEFINITION   Name: _Darnell_

WHAT I KNOW ABOUT THIS WORD

Vocabulary word:
climax

Part of speech:
noun

The text or quote where I first found the word:

Some critics argue that Ceasar's murder is not the climax of the story.

MY CLUES

Do I recognize any suffixes, prefixes, or root words?

max?

Does it remind me of other words?

climate? climb?

MAX means the most of something

Context clue #1:

probably a part of a story

Context clue #2:

some people think the murder isnt a climax so some people probably think it is

MY GUESS

My BEST GUESS definition (in my own words):

the most important part of a story

Last step: check your guess

Use a dictionary or glossary and write the correct definition:

the most intense or exciting part of a story; the turning point of a story

☒ I guessed right (or pretty close!)
☐ I guessed wrong. I'll re-read the passage with the correct definition in mind.

PREP TIME
You don't need to allow much preparation time for this activity. Identify a few sets of homonyms that you want to work on, including one for the mini-lesson example, and write up center instructions.

Homonym Sketches
Grades 4–12

Center(s)
Vocablulary

Skills
Students concentrate on the meanings of sound-alike words. They also improve their spelling and gain an important skill for independent vocabulary acquisition.

Mini-Lesson
Introduce this activity by explaining that homonyms are words that sound alike but are spelled differently and have different meanings. Because most students learn about homonyms in the primary grades, this will probably be a review. Continue by acknowledging that even experienced writers sometimes accidentally use the wrong word in a homonym pair – and experienced readers learn to look for context clues when they encounter a homonym in a text. Explain that the purpose of this activity is for students to create visual clues to help remind themselves "which word is which." Finally, model the activity by illustrating a pair of homonyms.

Overview
Students begin by brainstorming in small groups to create one or two sketches for each set of homonym words. After the learning centers, representatives from each group share their sketches with the entire class. Each student chooses

ENGAGING™
LEARNERS

the illustrations that they like best (that will help them remember the difference between the homonyms) and record them in their personal dictionary or vocabulary study guide.

Teacher Tips

This activity is a great way for content area teachers to address common misspellings. For example, a high school history teacher noticed that his students' assignments were plagued by *to-two-too* and *your-you're* errors. Rather than simply mark the mistakes on their papers, he included a Homonym Sketch center the next time he used Literacy & Learning Centers in his classroom.

The first time your class does this activity, prepare at least one extra pair of homonyms and model the activity by illustrating them during the mini-lesson.

If your content-specific vocabulary includes homonyms, be sure to include them in this activity. Social studies teachers might want to ask students to illustrate words like *isle/aisle* or *guerilla/gorilla*; science teachers might want to include *hail/hale*, *leach/leech*, or *pole/poll*; math teachers might want to have students illustrate the words *pi/pie* or *sine/sign*, etc.

Encourage students to focus their sketches on the letter(s) that are *different* between the words because that will help them remember the differences between the words.

You can either print the homonyms on worksheets or have students write the word groups themselves. If students write the words, their style of writing can be part of their visual clue.

When evaluating the sketches, be careful not to focus only on students' artistic abilities! Sometimes students have really useful memory tricks that they're able to describe even if they're unable to draw them well.

Center Prep

- Blank paper or worksheets with printed homonyms
- Pencils or writing implements
- Dictionaries, glossaries, or content-related texts (optional)
- Written center instructions
- Personal dictionaries or blank paper for students to create their own study guides after the full class discussion,

Representative List of Homonyms

ade/aid/aide	air/heir/err
ball/bawl	bare/bear
beat/beet	cell/sell
course/coarse	die/dye
find/fined	hall/haul
here/hear	him/hymn
hour/our	knew/new
know/no	lesson/lessen
one/won	pair/pare
peace/piece	profit/prophet
plain/plane	reign/rain
red/read	root/route
seen/scene	sight/site
some/sum	stare/stair
steal/steel	suite/sweet
tied/tide	to/two/too
wait/weight	would/wood
write/right	you're/your

HOMONYM SKETCHES
Sample Center Instructions

Provide written instructions at the center. Your instructions may look something like this sample. Feel free to adapt the instructions to suit your own needs.

1. Look at the groups of homonyms on the white board.

2. Choose one set of homonyms to start. You have **2 minutes** to discuss how you could best illustrate the difference between those words.
- Make sure everyone gets a chance to share their ideas!
- Assign a team member to use the dictionary if you need to look up a word meaning.

3. Assign one team member to sketch the illustration that your group agreed on. He/she has **1 minute** to draw the team's illustration.

4. Repeat with all 5 sets of homonyms, taking turns until you've all had a chance to contribute.

5. Assign a team member to keep your work. We'll be discussing it as a whole class by the end of the day.

You have permission to reproduce this page for use in your classroom.

  **ENGAGING™ LEARNERS**

HOMONYM SKETCHES
Example

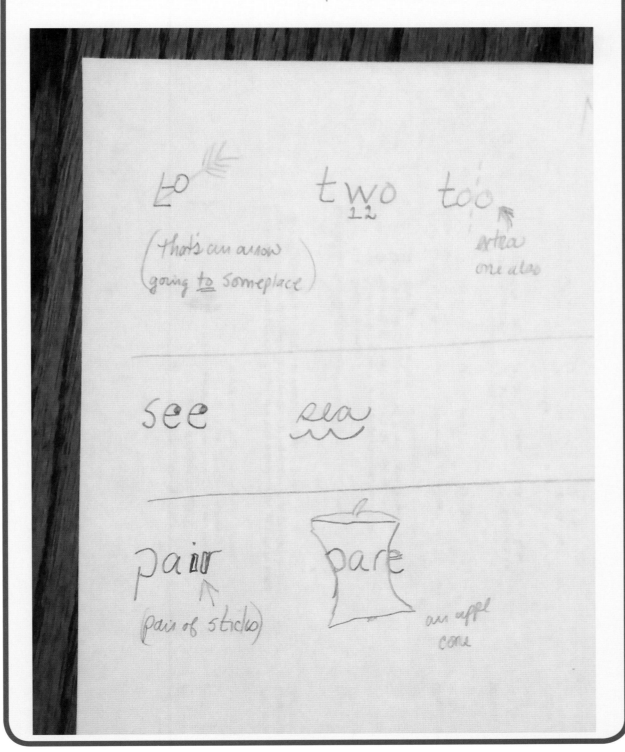

to *(that's an arrow going to someplace)*

two 1 2

too *extra one also*

see

sea

pair *(pair of sticks)*

pare *an apple core*

PREP TIME
Allow 1/2 to 1 hour the first time you do the activity because you'll need to write up center directions, prepare an example for the mini-lesson, and gather materials. After that, the activity more-or-less runs itself.

Lexicographer: Or Write Your Own Dictionary
Grades 4–12

Center(s)
Vocabulary

Skills
When they keep a personal record of newly acquired vocabulary words, students learn vocabulary as an aspect of self-directed and self-regulated learning. They practice using context clues and reference materials to determine word meanings, and they explore the relationship between word forms.

Activity Description
A lexicographer is someone who writes dictionary definitions. In this activity, students gather their own list of unfamiliar or unusual words during independent reading and, at the vocabulary center, enter them into their own personal dictionaries.

Mini-Lesson
When first introducing this activity, take a moment to describe what a lexicographer does. (They record the English language, as it is actually used, by writing and editing dictionary definitions.) Then explain that while they are not expected to record the entire English language, each student should attempt to record the words that he or she personally learns during the course of the semester or year. Model the activity by showing students an example of your

ENGAGING™ LEARNERS

own new word list. Then demonstrate how you look for context clues and research a word's correct definition. You may want to emphasize that the same words won't be new to everybody. Because of our various life experiences and reading backgrounds, different people know different words

Writing a personal dictionary is not competitive! While there's bound to be some overlap, every dictionary will have a different number of entries. And because students are writing definitions in their own words, they might vary from one dictionary to another. You may also want to do a quick review of different parts of speech if necessary.

Center Prep

- Students' personal dictionaries
- Students' personal word lists
- Pencils or pens
- Reference materials (dictionaries, online resources, glossaries, etc.)
- Written center instructions

Overview

Teachers in the primary grades often use personal dictionaries and word journals to give students an additional opportunity to engage with frequently used words, help with spelling, or to use as a resource when writing. The principle is the same but this activity adds a level of independence by encouraging students to come up with their own list of words.

The personal dictionary can easily be adapted for any classroom or content area. And if your school is practicing a whole-school literacy program, students can be encouraged to add words from all classes into one personal dictionary. This will give them an opportunity to see how language is related across disciplines and help them make new connections between content.

Step 1
Gather a Word List
This step can become an ongoing part of daily routine. Students should get in the habit of recording new words whenever they encounter them during independent or group reading, or as they listen to presentations. One of the easiest ways to do this is by using vocabulary bookmarks. You can offer students pre-printed bookmarks that have blanks for new words and a space to note where they were spotted. Older or more independent learners can simply keep a folded sheet of paper in each book or carry a small memo book with them to record new words. Each student should bring his/her own word lists to the vocabulary center.

Step 2
Research
Students use dictionaries, online resources, context clues, and textbook glossaries to determine the definitions of new words.

Step 3
Write Definitions
Each definition should include the word's part of speech: noun, verb, adjective, adverb, etc. Then a definition should be written in the student's own words. Finally, students should make a notation of where they first encountered the word.

Teacher Tips

Students can add illustrations to their definitions if desired. This is particularly useful for visual learners or if the dictionary is going to be used as a supplemental study aid. There are many ways to create dictionaries. Students can write definitions on index cards and file them alphabetically. Or, at the beginning of the school year or semester, they can label pages of a 60-page spiral-bound notebook with pages assigned to each letter. Because the frequency of initial letters varies (more words start with S than with Q, for example), you might want to assign the pages as indicated here. Feel free to change this as necessary depending on your discipline's vocabulary trends.

Letter	Number of pages	Letter	Number of pages
A	3	N	2
B	2	O	2
C	4	P	4
D	4	Q	1
E	2	R	2
F	2	S	5
G	2	T	2
H	2	U	2
I	2	V	2
J	2	W	2
K	2	X	1
L	2	Y	2
M	3	Z	1

Whenever it's appropriate, encourage student lexicographers to include possible word forms as part of the definition. For example, if they're defining *vertex* they can make a note that its plural form is *veritces*. If they're defining *diplomacy* they can make a note that *diplomatic* is the adjective form and that *diplomat* is someone who practices diplomacy.

This activity can serve as a great formative assessment tool. You might notice some students are encountering so many new words that they can't enter them all into their dictionaries. You might find that some students claim they aren't encountering new or unfamiliar words on a regular basis. In either case, work with the students to find differentiated texts. All students should be reading texts that are challenging, introducing them to new vocabulary and new ideas, but not so difficult that the students are frustrated.

Personal dictionaries can be kept in the classroom with other center work or students can carry them from class to class for easy reference. There are obvious advantages to giving students access to their dictionaries at any time, but if there's a good chance students will misplace or forget them, you may want to keep them safely in the classroom. Use whatever method works best for your situation.

Occasionally use this vocabulary center as an opportunity for students to share dictionaries with their group mates. They can discuss their favorite new words; add a classmate's word and definition to their own dictionary (it's not cheating or stealing, it's sharing knowledge!); or simply celebrate how many new words they've learned. This self-reflection is an important part of developing growth mindset in students and helps to create lifelong learners.

LEXICOGRAPHER: OR WRITE YOUR OWN DICTIONARY

Example: 7th Grade Science, Social Studies and ELA

Here is an example of a 7th grade student's personal dictionary. In this case, the student is creating one dictionary for all of his classes, with vocabulary from science, social studies, ELA and music in one place.

D

dialect (noun)
The way people talk in different places. Some of the folk tales are hard to understand because they're written in dialect.
English handout - October 12

desertification (noun)
turning farmland into a desert
Related word: desert
social studies Smithsonian website

dynamic (noun)
how loud or quiet you should sing
p means quiet and f means loud
music - Ms. Kwan says pay attention to dynamics

descending (adj)
getting smaller or going down
related word: descend (like stairs)
science - Mr. Watkins said it

E

exclave (noun)
When a country is surrounded!
Social studies - page 42 caption

equilateral (adj?)
all sides are same size
math book - page 77

VOCABULARY BOOKMARK

Date: 11/6 MONDAY
New word: finicky
Where found/heard: English class
Diary of Anne Frank talking about Ilse Wagner

Date: 11/6
New word: qualitative & quantitative
Where found/heard: science handout
These are probably opposites?

Date: 11/8 Wed.
New word: equation
Where found/heard: math p. 59
something about equal sign?

Date:
New word:
Where found/heard:

Date:
New word:
Where found/heard:

LEXICOGRAPHER: OR WRITE YOUR OWN DICTIONARY

VOCABULARY BOOKMARK

Date: _____
New word: _____
Where found/heard: _____
_____

Date: _____
New word: _____
Where found/heard: _____
_____

Date: _____
New word: _____
Where found/heard: _____
_____

Date: _____
New word: _____
Where found/heard: _____
_____

Date: _____
New word: _____
Where found/heard: _____
_____

VOCABULARY BOOKMARK

Date: _____
New word: _____
Where found/heard: _____
_____

Date: _____
New word: _____
Where found/heard: _____
_____

Date: _____
New word: _____
Where found/heard: _____
_____

Date: _____
New word: _____
Where found/heard: _____
_____

Date: _____
New word: _____
Where found/heard: _____
_____

VOCABULARY BOOKMARK

Date: _____
New word: _____
Where found/heard: _____
_____

Date: _____
New word: _____
Where found/heard: _____
_____

Date: _____
New word: _____
Where found/heard: _____
_____

Date: _____
New word: _____
Where found/heard: _____
_____

Date: _____
New word: _____
Where found/heard: _____
_____

You have permission to reproduce this page for use in your classroom.

ENGAGING™
LEARNERS

LEXICOGRAPHER: OR WRITE YOUR OWN DICTIONARY

VOCABULARY BOOKMARK

Date: _____
New word: _____
Where found/heard: _____

Date: _____
New word: _____
Where found/heard: _____

Date: _____
New word: _____
Where found/heard: _____

Date: _____
New word: _____
Where found/heard: _____

Date: _____
New word: _____
Where found/heard: _____

VOCABULARY BOOKMARK

Date: _____
New word: _____
Where found/heard: _____

Date: _____
New word: _____
Where found/heard: _____

Date: _____
New word: _____
Where found/heard: _____

Date: _____
New word: _____
Where found/heard: _____

Date: _____
New word: _____
Where found/heard: _____

VOCABULARY BOOKMARK

Date: _____
New word: _____
Where found/heard: _____

Date: _____
New word: _____
Where found/heard: _____

Date: _____
New word: _____
Where found/heard: _____

Date: _____
New word: _____
Where found/heard: _____

Date: _____
New word: _____
Where found/heard: _____

You have permission to reproduce this page for use in your classroom.

PREP TIME
The first time you use this activity you might need up to an 1 hour to choose prefixes, find vocabulary words for each prefix, create puzzle pieces, and print graphic organizers.

Prefix Puzzle
Grades 4-12

Center(s)
Vocabulary

Skills
Students explore academic and domain-specific vocabulary words while reinforcing their understanding of word construction. After completing the activity, they will be better prepared to independently analyze unfamiliar words and acquire new vocabulary.

Activity Description
This activity combines manipulation of physical puzzle pieces to support tactile or kinesthetic learners, with a graphic organizer and color cues to support visual learners. Students put together color-coded "puzzle pieces" to create words. Then they write the new words in a graphic organizer, and brainstorm other words that include the same prefixes.

Mini-Lesson
Introduce this activity by reviewing the use of prefixes. (Basically, a prefix is an affix – a letter or series of letters – that is placed before a root word or a word stem. Adding a prefix to the beginning of one word changes it into another word.) Then, review the meaning of the prefixes that are included in the activity. Finally, model the activity by putting together two same-colored puzzle pieces to create a word and adding the word to your sample graphic organizer.

ENGAGING™
LEARNERS

Overview

Step 1
Sort and combine
Students work in teams to sort puzzle pieces by color. They then combine pieces of the same color to form words. Allow each team to choose how they assign these tasks to team members.

Step 2
Transfer to Graphic Organizer
Students independently transfer the new words onto a graphic organizer. Each student completes his/her own graphic organizer.

Step 3
Find New Words
Students work in teams (discussing, brainstorming, or looking at glossaries/ dictionaries or content-related texts) to find other words that include the same prefixes. Each student records the team's words on his/her personal graphic organizer. Students are encouraged to keep their graphic organizer for reference or future study.

Teacher Tips

If students are keeping their own personal dictionaries, they can transfer new or unfamiliar words from their graphic organizer into their own dictionaries. Encourage them to make a note about the prefix and explain in their own words how it helped them to identify the word's meaning.

The first time your class does this activity, create at least one extra set of puzzle pieces and use that word as an example during the mini-lesson.

If you don't have access to colored paper, you can write words with colored markers on plain white paper.

Consider concluding the activity with a full-class discussion. Ask students if they noticed any patterns and what they may have learned about the different prefixes. Make a chart together, and record both what they learned about prefixes and any additional observations that they made about language.

Center Prep

- Prefix puzzle pieces:
    - Choose 3-5 prefixes to explore.
    - Find 2-4 vocabulary words for each of your chosen prefixes.
    - Create puzzle pieces by writing a prefix and a root word on slips of colored paper. It's most useful if you use a different colored paper for each prefix. For example: use red paper for all words starting with *pre* (*pre view*, *pre school*, etc.); use blue paper for all words starting with *sub* (*sub way*, *sub marine*, etc.); use green paper for all words starting with *mis* (*mis take*, *mis understand*, etc.)
- Printed Prefix Puzzle graphic organizers (one for each student)
- Pencils or writing implements
- Dictionaries, glossaries, or content-related texts (optional)
- Written center instructions

Adjusting the Rigor

If you're working with younger or struggling learners, you can limit the number of prefixes. For example, adapt this activity to only explore words that begin with one prefix. The next time you do the activity, explore a different prefix.

Experienced or older students enjoy finding words and creating puzzle pieces for their peers. Give them an opportunity to search content-related texts for words that include prefixes. (Make sure they check each word in a dictionary or other reference to confirm that it actually uses a prefix, because there are imposters! For example: the word *pretty* starts with *pre*, but that doesn't mean it is constructed with a prefix.)

PREFIX PUZZLE
Sample Center Instructions

1. **Work togethe**r to sort the puzzle pieces by color. You should have 4 red pieces, 4 blue pieces, 4 yellow pieces, and 4 green pieces.

2. **Work together** to combine prefixes and root words/word stems to create 8 words. (Blue prefixes go with blue root words, red prefixes go with red root words, etc.)

3. **Work independently** to complete the first 3 columns of your own Prefix Puzzle graphic organizer. Use the 8 words that you just created with the puzzle pieces.

4. **Work together** to think of additional words that start with the same prefixes. You can look through your independent reading book if you want to find words. Write them in the last column of your graphic organizer.

5. Keep your completed graphic organizer in your folder! We'll use it tomorrow.

ENGAGING™
LEARNERS

PREFIX PUZZLE

Here is an example of an activity as done in an 6th grade ELA class. During a large-group discussion after the activity, the teacher took the opportunity to encouraged the whole class to think of other words that use the in- prefix.

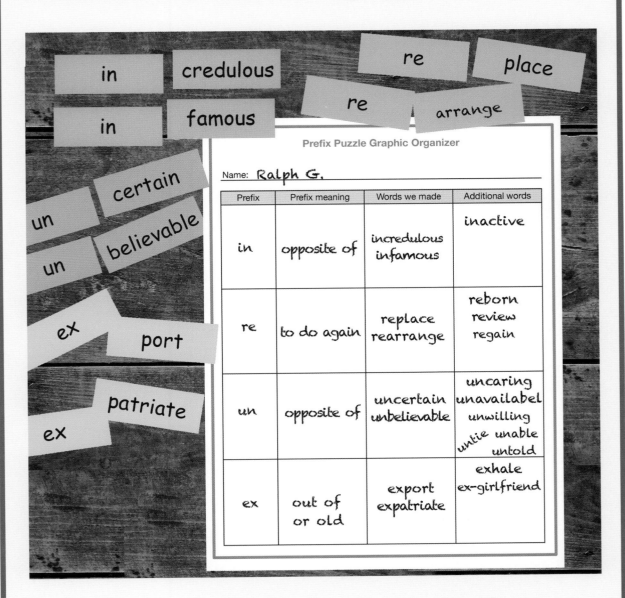

Prefix Puzzle Graphic Organizer

Name: Ralph G.

Prefix	Prefix meaning	Words we made	Additional words
in	opposite of	incredulous infamous	inactive
re	to do again	replace rearrange	reborn review regain
un	opposite of	uncertain unbelievable	uncaring unavailabel unwilling untie unable untold
ex	out of or old	export expatriate	exhale ex-girlfriend

PREFIX PUZZLE

This is an example of puzzle pieces as they were prepared for use in a high school AP Biology class review session. As you can see, the Prefix Puzzle activity is easily adapted for use in content-area classes.

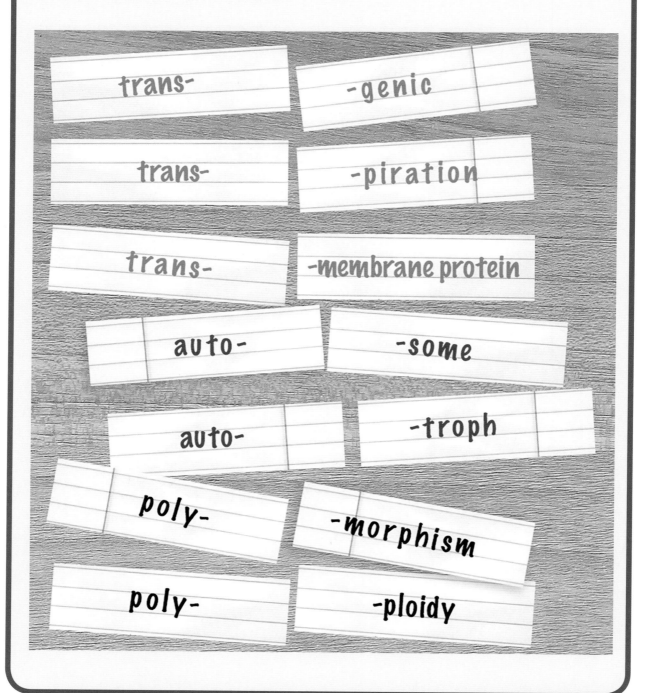

PREFIX PUZZLE
Graphic Organizer

Prefix Puzzle Graphic Organizer

Name: _____

Prefix	Prefix meaning	Words we made	Additional words

You have permission to reproduce this page for use in your classroom.

Vocabulary Carousel
Grades 4-12

Center(s)
Vocabulary

Skills
Students develop word knowledge and descriptive language.

Overview
This lesson creates the opportunity to generate lists of synonyms to develop students' word knowledge. This activity will also prompt the student speaker/writer to go beyond the most commonly used words an choose options that more precisely match their thoughts. As an optional follow-up to the vocabulaary carousel activity, instruct students to record the new words in their personal dictionaries for future reference.

Mini-Lesson
Even though the English language includes many words that mean the same thing – or almost the same thing! – explain that good writers try to choose the exact word that expresses their precise meaning. For example, the word *proposed* is slightly different from the word *suggested*. The word *obsolete* has different implications than the more common word, *old*. The students' goal is to have a big vocabulary so they can say and write exactly what they mean.

Center Prep

- Write a different vocabulary word in the center circle of 4 or 5 printed Blank Vocabulary Carousel sheets. You'll need enough for each rotation. For example, if you have four groups of 5 students, you'll print 20 Blank Vocabulary Carousel sheets.
- At least 4 or 5 different colored pens or pencils (one for each student at the center)
- Dictionary and/or thesaurus (optional)
- Timer
- Written center instructions

Activity Description

Step 1
Each student chooses a different colored pencil/pen (so that their work can be identified).

Step 2
Each student starts with a Blank Vocabulary Carousel sheet. The timer is set and they have one minute (or a period of time that you think is appropriate) to fill in the empty top circle with synonyms for the word that has been written in the center circle. When the timer goes off, each student passes their sheet to their right.

Step 3
Set the timer for one more minute. The students fill in the next blank circle with synonyms for the new word in the center circle. They are not allowed to repeat a word that their teammate has already written.

Step 4
Repeat until the Vocabulary Carousel sheets have made it all the way around the group – like a carousel – and all students have had a chance to write at least one synonym for each word.

Step 5
In the remaining time, students can use dictionaries, glossaries, etc. to find more synonyms. If necessary, they can look up the definition of the center vocabulary word and complete the corresponding Vocabulary Carousel sheet as a team. Remember, the objective is for each person to write as many unique synonyms for each center word as possible.

Teacher Tips
See the related Adjective Carousel activity to see how this activity can be adapted to refresh students' understanding of different parts of speech.

Feel free to use vocabulary from relevant content-area texts!

Adjusting the Rigor
Challenge students to choose one of the words and a student-supplied synonym. Ask them to describe the ways in which they mean the same thing, and ask them to identify subtle differences in meaning. Encourage them to provide examples if possible. (For example, a student might say, "Obsolete things are usually old, but some old things are not obsolete because so many people still use them. For example, spoons have been around for a long time but they're not really obsolete because we haven't really invented anything better yet.")

VOCABULARY CAROUSEL
Graphic Organizer

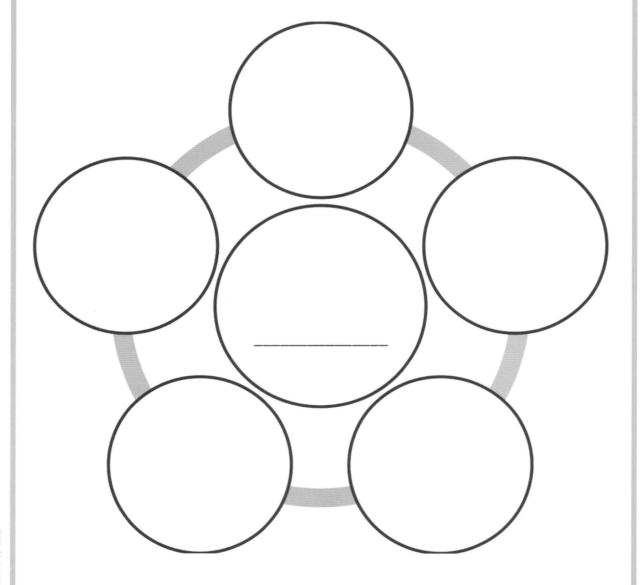

ENGAGING™ LEARNERS

VOCABULARY CAROUSEL
Sample Center Instructions

Provide written instructions at the center. Your instructions may look something like this sample. Feel free to adapt this to suit your classroom's needs.

1. Choose a colored pencil. Everyone pick a different color.

2. Grab a packet of Vocabulary Carousel sheets. Each packet is paper-clipped together. Divide them up. Everyone in your group will start with a different sheet.

3. **Set the timer for 1 minute**. You each have one minute to fill in one circle with as many synonyms for the vocabulary word (the word in the center circle) as you can think of. Don't use the dictionary or thesaurus yet! That's the last step.

4. When the timer goes off, everyone pass his/her sheet to the right. **Set the timer for 1 minute**. You now have one minute to fill in the next circle with as many synonyms for the word in the center circle of this new Vocabulary Carousel sheet. DON'T WRITE A WORD THAT HAS ALREADY BEEN WRITTEN!

5. Repeat the process until everyone has had a chance to work on every Vocabulary Carousel sheet. Remember to **set the timer for 1 minute each time**.

6. There will be time left over. Use this time to discuss your work and brainstorm additional words. AS A GROUP you can now look words up in the dictionary or thesaurus. Add any new synonyms you come up with to the sheets. Maybe you already thought of all the best ones!

7. END OF CENTER – Clip all five Vocabulary Carousel sheets together and keep them in your group folder. The whole class will discuss them on Monday and we'll add the best ones to our personal dictionaries.

Notes on this Chapter

Chapter 6

Tools for Writer's Craft Centers

PREP TIME
It usually takes less than 1/2 hour to gather materials and write up center instructions.

Lists of Ten
Grades 4-12

Center(s)
Writer's Craft

Skills
This activity encourages students to independently plan for future routine writing activities, with an eye toward various tasks, purposes, and audiences.

Center Prep
- Manila folders or sheets of construction paper to create folders
- Tape, staplers, markers, as needed to create or decorate writing folders
- Written center instructions

Mini-Lesson
Tell your students that they are creating writing folders to hold any and all writing that they do during the year: good stuff, bad stuff, ideas, partly finished pieces, finished work - any writing at all. Explain too that the writing folder is a personal and private file for the student's eyes only. Then explain that the purpose of a writing prompt is to inspire a writer and to give him/her something to write about. By having a list of prompts prepared in advance, a writer will never have to worry about having nothing to write about.

Overview

Writing can be so intimidating, but it doesn't have to be! Young writers often complain that they have no idea what to write about when they are given an opportunity to write freely about anything they care to. Here is a quick scaffolding idea to help your students always have interesting topics on hand.

First, have students create writing folders. Have them decorate the manila folders or create their own folders from the sheets of construction paper and then decorate them. Next, ask your students to make a list of ten items for each of five categories.

When the students have their lists in hand, ask them to staple or glue the lists on the inside of their writing folder's front cover. The next time they say they have nothing to write about, refer them to their Lists of Ten, where they will find at least fifty fresh ideas.

Teacher Tips

For the greatest impact, do this activity early in the school year or at the start of a new semester.

Because this activity may take several center rotations to complete, you may want to divide the steps up over a few days.

Adjusting the Rigor

Older and more experienced student writers can be encouraged to pre-write topic sentences for the items on their lists. Remind them that these sentences are for inspiration only, and they can revise them or completely change them before actually using the writing prompts. So on their list of Ten Successful Atheletes, they could write things like: "Wilma Rudolph deserves to be more famous," and "He succeeded at getting rich but Lance Armstrong was a cheater."

Notes

_____
_____
_____
_____
_____
_____
_____
_____
_____
_____
_____
_____
_____
_____
_____
_____
_____
_____
_____
_____
_____
_____
_____
_____
_____
_____
_____
_____
_____
_____

LISTS OF TEN
Examples

Teachers that use the Writer's Craft center to focus on creative writing can use categories like:

- Ten people I'd really like to have dinner with
- Ten amazing songs
- Ten delicious foods
- Ten places I'd like to visit
- Ten favorite books
- Ten characters from books that I would like to know personally
- Ten favorite games
- Ten goals for the future
- Ten activities I could write detailed instructions for
- Ten animals that scare me
- Ten things I want but that I couldn't buy with a billion dollars

Ten important things I'd like to learn about. Content area classes can be more specific by including categories like:

- Ten illustrations from the text book that look especially interesting (even if I don't know what they mean yet!)
- Ten ways life would be different without science
- Ten successful Olympic athletes
- Ten historical events I wish I had attended (look at your supplemental photograph book for ideas)
- Ten things I want to learn about the oceans
- Ten crops or animals I think I'd like to raise on my farm someday
- Ten favorite postcards from the 20th Century Asia bulletin board
- Ten things I'd include if I wrote an Algebra 2 textbook
- Ten things I'd do if I were the first person on Mars
- Ten most interesting people from the American Civil War
- Ten endangered species
- Ten ways a robot could be helpful to me

You get the idea. It's very unlikely that students will ever write about all of the items on their Lists of Ten. The goal is to give them a wide range of prompts for various Writer's Craft center and independent writing activities throughout the semester or school year.

Remind students that many professional writers keep journals and notebooks with an on-going "life list" of writing prompts. Invite them to add to their lists any time they find new or inspiring topics.

ENGAGING™ LEARNERS

PREP TIME
It might take up to 1 hour to find a compound or complex sentence from your content area. As you gain familiarity with the activity, you'll save time by finding examples during routine reading. Allow time to write up center directions and prepare mini-lesson example.

Break It Up Yourself
Grades 4-12

Center(s)
Writer's Craft

Skills
Practice isolating ideas in a compound or complex sentence while reviewing content. Gain experience in writing, textual analysis, exploring text structure, style choice, and grammar.

Overview
Complex and compound sentences often intimidate struggling or less experienced readers and writers. Give students an opportunity to practice "breaking up" a long sentence into multiple short sentences that will make it easier for readers to understand their meaning.

This writing strategy is easily adapted to both ELA and content-area classrooms. It can be used alone at the Writer's Craft center, or in tandem with the BREAK IT UP activity at the Reading Together center (see Chapter 4).

Teacher Tips

If you're unsure how to create simple sentences out of a complex sentence, let the punctuation tip you off. Commas, semicolons, dashes, and parentheses – as well as "connecting words" like *and, but,* and *or* – are hints that a long sentence could be broken up into little sentences! For more information about compound and complex sentences,

visit this helpful website:
quickanddirtytips.com/grammar-girl.
(Mignon Fogarty is Grammar Girl. Her easy to understand explanations make sense to people who aren't English teachers.)

Mini-Lesson

Model the activity by "breaking up" a complex or compound sentence into short, simple sentences. Remind students that punctuation, and conjunctions ("connecting words" like *and*, *but*, and *or*) can serve as clues. They are often used to connect separate thoughts in a complex sentence. Demonstrate that the words in the original complex sentence might have to be rearranged in order to create well-formed simple sentences.

Center Prep

- Find a compound/complex sentence related to your content or from your current reading. Type or write it out, one copy for each group.
- A graphic organizer, one for each group (You can substitute blank paper if you want.)
- Colored pencils
- Written center instructions

Activity Description

Step 1
Students read (or attempt to read) the compound/complex sentence together.

Step 2
Students take turns writing short, simple sentences based on ideas that are found in the compound/complex sentence. They are encouraged to discuss their reasoning with other group members.

BREAK IT UP YOURSELF
Sample Center Instructions

AS A GROUP
Read the complex sentence. It's from one of this week's Learn More challenge readings. It includes a lot of information and many ideas!

Take turns identifying single ideas that are expressed in the complex sentence.

INDIVIDUALLY
Choose a colored pencil. Everyone use a different color!

Write one short, simple sentence stating the single idea you identified from the complex sentence.

Discuss spelling, punctuation, and grammar. Do your best work. Help each other!

Examine the complex sentence closely and find the idea represented by your simple sentence.

Use your colored pencil to underline the part of the complex sentence that is the source for your simple sentence.

Hint: The parts of your simple sentence (subject, verb, object) might not be "all in a row" in the complex sentence. And sometimes the ideas are implied rather than stated, so you might have to really look hard!

BREAK IT UP YOURSELF
Example: Science

Complex sentence

Continental Drift: Theory & Definition
By Becky Oskin, Contributing Writer | February 4, 2015

Set forth in 1912 by Alfred Wegener, a geophysicist and meteorologist, continental drift

also explained why look-alike animal and plant fossils, and similar rock formations,

are found on different continents.

https://www.livescience.com/37529-continental-drift.html

Your name:	Your simple sentence:
Marisa	Alfred Wegener was a geophysicist and meteorologist.
Nick	The theory of continental drift was set forth in 1912.
Dara	Continental drift was set forth by Alfred Wegener.
Matthew C.	Look-alike animal and plant fossils are found on different continents.
Aja	Continental drift explained why similar rock formations are found on different continetnts.

ENGAGING™ LEARNERS

BREAK IT UP YOURSELF
Graphic Organizer

Complex sentence

Your name:	Your simple sentence:
Your name:	Your simple sentence:
Your name:	Your simple sentence:
Your name:	Your simple sentence:
Your name:	Your simple sentence:

You have permission to reproduce this page for use in your classroom.

PREP TIME
This activity doesn't require much advance preparation. It usually takes about 1/2 hour to write center instructions, prepare for the mini-lesson, and print graphic organizers.

Panel of Experts
Grades 4-12

Center(s)
Writer's Craft

Skills
Express and explore multiple points of view. Integrate point of view and voice into writing.

Overview
Observers walking by your classroom door might think you've given your students the day off but you'll actually be engaging in an activity that encourages them to develop oral communication, team building, self-awareness, self-confidence, critical and creative problem solving, and idea generation.

Teacher Tips
Students can also play Panel of Experts as a Speaking & Listening center activity.

Panel of Experts would also be a perfect activity when classes resume in January, as an engaging way to jump-start a new unit or help students brush-up on content.

ENGAGING™ LEARNERS

Mini-Lesson

Begin by playing the Panel of Experts as a full-class exercise. See an explanation of this activity on the next page.

Center Prep

- Print the Panel of Experts graphic organizer (one for each student.
- Timer (optional)
- Written center instructions

Activity Description

After the students have participated in Panel of Experts full-class activity, use the information that the students gained from the different points of view for a writing activity.

Notes

_____
_____
_____
_____
_____
_____
_____
_____
_____
_____
_____
_____
_____
_____
_____
_____

PANEL OF EXPERTS
Sample Center Instructions

Provide written instructions at the center. Your instructions may look something like this sample. Feel free to adapt this to suit your classroom's needs.

1. Complete the graphic organizer and record the different points of view that you heard in the Panel of Experts mini-lesson.

2. Discuss with your group the points of view that you all heard in the Panel of Experts mini-lesson. Did you all hear exactly the same thing? (Hint: probably not!)

3. Using your graphic organizer, write a summary of the topic or subject from one point of view. This summary should be one paragraph (3–5 sentences) long.

PANEL OF EXPERTS
Full-Class Activity

In this exercise, a student group plays a panel of experts to answer questions from their teacher and classmates.

The activity can be adapted so that the experts are asked to explore/review content (in science, math, technology, social studies, or humanities classes), or plot, point of view, or character (in literature class).

Instructions

- Invite three to six players into the playing area. Players sit in chairs facing the audience of remaining students.

- The teacher assigns an area of expertise for each member on the panel. One traditional way to do this is to ask the audience simple questions and use their answers as the areas of expertise.

- Ask each expert to introduce herself with a brief statement about her area of expertise.

- The host (teacher) asks the panel questions and prompts each expert to answer in turn.

- After a couple of questions, the audience may ask questions.

Teacher Tips

After students are familiar with the game, a student can act as the host and the teacher can facilitate and observe.

If you're using the exercise to review or explore specific curricular content, experts can be assigned as different systems of the body, experts in different periods of history, etc. Experts can also be famous scientists or characters in a novel.

This material is reproduced with permission of John Wiley & Sons, Inc.
McKnight, Katherine S., and Mary Scruggs. The Second City Guide to Improv
in the Classroom: Using Improvisation to Teach Skills and Boost Learning.
San Francisco, CA: Jossey-Bass, 2008.

  **ENGAGING™ LEARNERS**

PANEL OF EXPERTS
Graphic Organizer

Name: _____

Date: _____

As you watch Panel of Experts, record the different points of view that are represented. Record corresponding details and information for each point of view. Use this information to draft a written summary of the presented information.

PANEL OF EXPERTS

	Name of expert	What is their viewpoint?	What details and evidence does the expert provide to support their viewpoint?
Expert one			
Expert two			
Expert three			
Expert four			

You have permission to reproduce this page for use in your classroom.

PREP TIME
At first you might need up to 1 hour to find sentences that are appropriate for translation. As you gain familiarity with the activity, you'll save a lot of time by finding examples during routine reading.

Text Translator
Grades 4-12

Center(s)
Writer's Craft

Skills
Students gain skills in word choice, and differentiating between writing for different tasks/purposes/audiences. They also practice reading skills like summarization, word choice analysis, and text structure; and grammar skills like spelling, punctuation, and capitalization.

Overview
Students translate a piece of writing from the standard (or academic) language in which it was written, into "Text Speak" and back again.

Mini-Lesson
Model this activity by reading a Text Speak message and translating it into standard, academic English. Then brainstorm as a class to translate a short piece of literature or academic writing into Text Speak. Tip: Start with one or two sentences. Allow students to come up with different spellings and abbreviations.

Activity Description
Students translate short pieces of academic text or literature into Text Speak. Then they translate each others' texts back into standard English.

Center Prep

- Write a selection of sentences on slips of paper. These can be from textbooks or other source material that the students are reading.
- Writing materials (paper, pencils, etc.)
- Timer (optional)
- Written center instructions

Teacher Tip

Follow-up conversations after completing the activity can include full-class discussions of the advantages of both kinds of writing. Text Speak is quicker (fewer key strokes), fun, and a good way to communicate between people who share a common background. Standard English generally allows for more specificity of thought and allows people to communicate across different social groups and times (slang changes quickly).

Adjusting the Rigor

You can ask students to work on a short paragraph instead of a single sentence.

Notes
_____
_____
_____
_____
_____
_____
_____
_____
_____

TEXT TRANSLATOR
Sample Center Instructions

Provide written instructions at the center. Feel free to adapt this to suit your classroom's needs.

1. **Pull a slip of paper out of the bag.** Each student pulls one sentence but don't show each other what you got!

2. **Translate.** You have 2 minutes to translate your sentence from Standard English into Text Speak. Write your new text on an index card. You can only use characters that you'd find on a phone. Emojis, letters, numbers and punctuation are ok; pictures are not ok.

3. **Trade texts.** Give your Text Speak message to the person on your right.

4. **Translate.** You have 2 minutes to translate the Text Speak message into Standard English. Write your new Standard English sentence on the back of the index card. You can only use letters, numbers, and punctuation. Emojis and pictures are not ok.

5. **Discuss.** You have 4 minutes to discuss results. (Keep your voices low!) Answer these questions:

- How close did you get? Did you translate the text back to the original Standard English sentence?

- Which was easier to understand, the sentence or the Text Speak message?

- Were you able to spell the words correctly when you wrote Standard English?

- Did you guess the correct punctuation when you wrote Standard English?

- How important is the spelling and punctuation? Would the meaning change if you guessed wrong?

PREP TIME
The first time you use this activity you may need up to 1 hour to find or write run-on sentences - especially if you're not familiar with the grammar rules.

Stopping Run-Ons
Grades 4-12

Center(s)
Writer's Craft
Reading Together
Grammar

Skills
Students gain practice in revising and editing while reinforcing their understanding of punctuation and capitalization. In order to complete the task, they have to do simple textual analysis of the supplied "run-on" sentence in order to make the correct editing choices.

Activity Description
Students edit one long, run-on sentence to create a series of shorter, grammatically-correct sentences.

Mini-Lesson
Review the definition of complete, grammatically-correct sentences. Compare them to run-on or fused sentences. Model the tools writers can use to repair run-on sentences: commas, semicolons, commas with appropriate conjunctions – or run-ons can just be divided up into shorter sentences by adding periods and capitalization.

For more information about run-on sentences, visit this helpful website: **quickanddirtytips.com/grammar-girl**.

ENGAGING™
LEARNERS

Overview

Stopping Run-Ons is one of my favorite center activities because:

- It combines active reading with grammar skill reinforcement.

- It reminds students of the importance of clearly written communication in all subject areas.

- It encourages students to read content closely, while paying attention to the meaning of each individual sentence.

- It's easily adapted to both ELA and content-area classrooms!

All you need is a sample text that includes run-on sentences. You can write these yourself, adapt them from texts that relate to your content, or re-write texts that your students are already studying. You could even choose a passage from a textbook and rewrite it to include run-on sentences.

Adjusting the Rigor

If you have a few students who are quick to master this skill, ask them each to create a run-on sentence from well-written text. Then they can trade sentences with each other and practice rewriting the run-on into short, grammatically-correct sentences. After that step is complete, invite the students to compare their short sentences to the author's original writing. Are they exactly the same? Is the meaning exactly the same or has it changed slightly? If there are differences, invite the students to discuss the possible reasons. As readers, were they forced to make assumptions when they analyzed the run-on sentence? Are shorter sentences always easier to understand?

Notes

_____
_____
_____
_____
_____
_____
_____
_____
_____
_____
_____
_____
_____
_____
_____
_____
_____
_____
_____
_____
_____
_____
_____
_____
_____
_____

STOPPING RUN-ONS
Example: Social Studies

The sample Literacy & Learning Center activity below shows how this grammar activity was adapted for use in a 5th grade Social Studies class. The teacher wrote this run-on sentence herself in order to reinforce one of the unit's most important themes.

Team: _Mike   Tessa   Moe_

This is a run-on sentence:

Lewis and Clark's team opened the way for the colonization of the western United States their maps and journals helped other explorers and settlers move west.

Write two grammatically correct sentences:

Lewis and Clark's team opened the way for the colonization of the western United States.
Their maps and journals helped other explorers and settlers move west.

ENGAGING™ LEARNERS

STOPPING RUN-ONS
Example: Environmental Science

The sample Literacy & Learning Center activity below shows how this grammar activity was adapted for use in a high school Environmental Science class.
In this case, the student teams were asked to make their punctuation/capitalization notations directly on a supplied handout.

AS A GROUP
- **Read** the following paragraph about sea level rise on Pacific coast. It consists of one, long, run-on sentence!
- **Add punctuation and capitalization** to change the run-on into three complete sentences.

OPTIONAL
- If you want to read the rest of the article individually - at home or during free reading time - it will be bookmarked on the classroom web page. By the way, the real article is very well written and doesn't contain any run-ons!

NEWSWAVE – News from the U.S. Department of the Interior, Winter 2016

"Marshes to Mudflats—New Study: By 2110 Sea-Level Rise Will Drown Most Wetlands Along Oregon and Washington Coasts" by Karen Thorne, Ryan McClymont (USGS)

Tidal marshes provide habitat for endangered wildlife and protect coastal communities from flooding. a new report from the USGS suggests that Oregon and Washington may lose most of these habitats in the next century. although their models showed most marshlands will remain during the next 50–70 years, scientists predict that none of the wetlands will build up enough sediment to outpace sea-level rise and consequently will convert to mudflats by 2110.

https://www.doi.gov/sites/doi.gov/files/uploads/NEWSWAVE_Winter2016.pdf#page=8

Notes on this Chapter

Chapter 7
Tools for Grammar Centers

PREP TIME
Allow time to craft sentence fragments and write up center instructions. It might take a little longer if you need to refresh your understanding of complete sentences vs. sentence fragments.

Defragging Sentence Fragments
Grades 4-12

Center(s)
Grammar
Writer's Craft

Skills
Students practice recognizing the difference between sentence fragments and complete sentences. They then craft complete sentences to express clear ideas about content.

Mini-Lesson
Remind students that a complete sentence consists of two parts, a subject and a predicate. These two parts combine to express a complete thought.

If your students struggle with this concept, you might want to display a graphic to illustrate the idea.

Remind the students that a written sentence always begins with a capital letter and concludes with end punctuation - a period, question mark, or exclamation point.

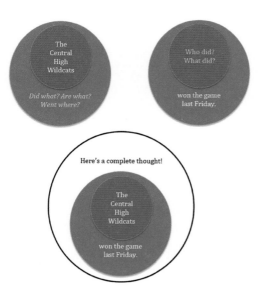

ENGAGING™ LEARNERS

Center Prep

- Sentence subjects and predicates, written on individual slips of paper
- Writing material (paper/pencils, etc.)
- Written center instructions

Overview

In this activity, students match up two sentence fragments to create one complete sentence.

Start by creating simple sentences about your subject matter. Take these from a textbook, a supplemental reading, a primary source document, or write them yourself. For the purpose of this activity, it's best to keep the sentences as simple as possible. Remove extra clauses and unnecessary modifiers.

Prepare for the activity by writing subjects and predicates on individual slips of paper. During the center activity, students will match up the sentence fragments to create complete sentences. Combined sentence fragments will be handwritten as complete sentences using correct capitalization and punctuation. See the example on the next page of the Defragging Sentence Fragments activity from a middle school physical science class.

Teacher Tip

Create a rough draft in which you divide the sentences up into subjects and predicates. Remove all capitalization and punctuation. Proofread your fragments and make sure there is only one correct option for each match-up.

DEFRAGGING SENTENCE STATEMENTS
Sample Center Instructions

Provide written instructions at the center. Your instructions may look something like this sample.
Feel free to adapt this to suit your classroom's needs.

1. Dump the sentence fragment slips out of the envelope and turn them all right-side-up.

2. Work as a team to pair them up. Your goal is to create TRUE sentences!

3. Check your work! Refer to Chapter 6 in the textbook.

4. Did you make any mistakes? If so, fix them! Discuss why you made the mistake. Is there anything you can do the help you remember the right information?

5. Write one complete, true sentence for each pair of sentence fragments.

6. Keep a copy of your group's complete sentences your folder. It will help you review for next Friday's quiz!

DEFRAGGING SENTENCE STATEMENTS
Example: Physical Science

Prepare for the activity by writing subjects and predicates on individual slips of paper. During the center activity, students will match up the sentence fragments to create complete sentences. Then students will write the combined sentence fragments as complete sentences using correct capitalization and punctuation. See this sample of the activity taken from a middle school physical science class:

a completed circuit

turns the electromagnet on

electromagnets

can be turned on and off

Bruce, Juanita, Nico, Sam

Electromagnets can be turned on and off.

A completed circuit turns the electromagnet on.

Permanent magnets are made from "hard" ferromagnetic materials.

An interrupted circuit turns the electromagnet off.

The south end of one magnet attracts the north end of another magnet.

permanent magnets

are made from "hard" ferromagnetic materials

an interrupted circuit

turns the electromagnet off

the south end of one magnet

attracts the north end of another magnet

ENGAGING™ LEARNERS

Ready to introduce Literacy & Learning Centers in your school?

Need hands-on support?

Contact us at
info@EngagingLearners.com
or call **(312) 576-8222**

to schedule a free, no-obligation phone consultation with Dr. McKnight

The Engaging Learners team can come to YOU!

We work with school leadership to create customized professional development to address each school's unique challenges. Whether you're looking for a 1-day presentation, a hands-on workshop, or on-going support, our PD leaders will help your teachers achieve amazing literacy growth. Visit **www.EngagingLearners.com/on-site** for more info.

PREP TIME

It doesn't usually take long to find an appropriate content-related text. The first time you use the activity you'll need to allow time to write up center instructions.

Gathering Common Nouns
Grades 4–12

Center(s)

Grammar

Skills

Students learn to distinguish between common nouns and proper nouns and practice differentiating parts of speech. This activity can also be used to help with vocabulary review or acquisition.

Overview

This center activity gives students a chance to practice identifying common nouns. As they explore a text, object, or location (like a lab, classroom, or field trip destination), students practice identifying this part of speech in both its singular and plural forms. Throughout the activity students are encouraged to work as a team and check each other's work.

Activity Description

Step 1

Each group chooses a member to be the recorder. The recorder will be the team member who writes the nouns onto the correct worksheet as the team finds them.

Step 2
Start with singular common nouns. Students read a pre-selected text together and begin identifying singular common nouns. Encourage students to express their reasoning (Why is this word a common noun instead of a proper noun? How do you know it is singular? Do you know what the plural form might be?). The recorder can only write a word on the blank Singular Common Nouns worksheet if the entire group agrees that it belongs there.

Step 3
Students choose a different team member to act as the recorder.

Step 4
The group takes a blank Plural Common Noun work sheet and repeats the process by examining the pre-selected text and identifying plural common nouns. The recorder writes the agreed upon words onto the worksheet.

Center Prep

- A text that includes lots of singular and plural common nouns (this can be from a textbook or any supplemental reading material)
- Blank worksheets, one for singular common nouns and one for plural common nouns (or provide blank paper and let groups make their own)
- Pencils/pens
- Written center instructions

Mini-Lesson

Introduce this activity by reminding the class that nouns are one of the eight parts of speech. Although the activity is only concerned with common nouns, this is a good opportunity to explain the difference between common nouns and proper nouns, giving examples of each.
For example:

- Common nouns begin with a lowercase letter and name non-specific persons, places, things or ideas. Proper nouns begin with an uppercase letter and name a specific person, place, thing or idea.
- Both common nouns and proper nouns can be plural or singular. Singular means there is one of something and plural means there are more than one.

Examples:

- **The girl went to the lake.**
  Girl and *lake* are singular common nouns. There is just one girl and one lake, but we don't know which girl and we don't know which lake.

- **Shasta went to Lake Geneva.**
  Shasta and *Lake Geneva* are singular proper nouns; we know the name of the one girl and we know which one lake she visited.

- **The basketball players ate some cookies.**
  Both *players* and *cookies* are plural common nouns. We don't know who the players are, but we know there is more than one of them; we don't know what kind of cookies they ate, but we know they ate more than one cookie.

- **The Centerville Flyers ate some Oreos.**
  Both *Centerville Flyers* and *Oreos* are plural proper nouns. We know which players the sentence is talking about and we know what brand of cookie they ate.

Teacher Tips

Consider using this grammar activity as part of a vocabulary review. For example, an Industrial Arts teacher could ask students to examine a tool, like a bandsaw, and identify the common nouns that describe its parts: switch, blade guard, knobs, guides, etc. Those common nouns could be contrasted with proper nouns that might be found in the classroom: Shop-Vac (a brand name wet/dry vacuum cleaner), Workmate (a brand name workbench/sawhorse), etc.

This center activity was adapted from a whole-class activity in which the teacher hangs a sheet of butcher paper labeled *Singular Common Nouns* in the front of the classroom, and one labeled *Plural Common Nouns* in the back of the classroom. The class is divided into two teams and given 2 minutes to write all of the common nouns they notice in the classroom. (The team working on singular common nouns writes words like: *book, floor, light, desk*, etc. The team working on plural common nouns writes words like: *pencils, desks, backpacks*, etc.) After 2 minutes the teams switch places. When the activity is complete the whole class compares the *Singular* and *Plural* lists and identifies those words that are related. (Desks is the plural form of desk, for example.) This whole-class activity can be used as a low-pressure introduction to the center activity.

It's typical for students to include adjectives (words that describe nouns) as part of common nouns: *geography* book, *on/off* switch, *soccer* coach, and *tissue* box, for example. You might want to prepare to discuss adjectives as a different part of speech in case that happens.

Adjusting the Rigor

Students who have already mastered this skill, or who master it quickly, can be invited to take it a step further by identifying common nouns while listening to a recorded speech or a text. You can do this version of the activity at a combined listening/grammar station.

Note that when they listen to a text, the students will not have the visual cue of uppercase/lowercase letters to help them distinguish between common and proper nouns.

By adapting this activity to exploring objects or physical environments (like a classroom, lab, or field trip destination), struggling or less experienced readers are able to practice part-of-speech recognition independent of their reading abilities.

Notes

_____
_____
_____
_____
_____
_____
_____
_____
_____
_____
_____
_____

ENGAGING™ LEARNERS

GATHERING COMMON NOUNS
Example: American Literature Class (10th Grade)

A literature teacher could incorporate this Gathering Common Nouns Literacy & Learning Center activity into a class reading of the novel, *The Scarlet Letter*. Students would have the opportunity to identify of parts of speech while learning vocabulary and exploring text.

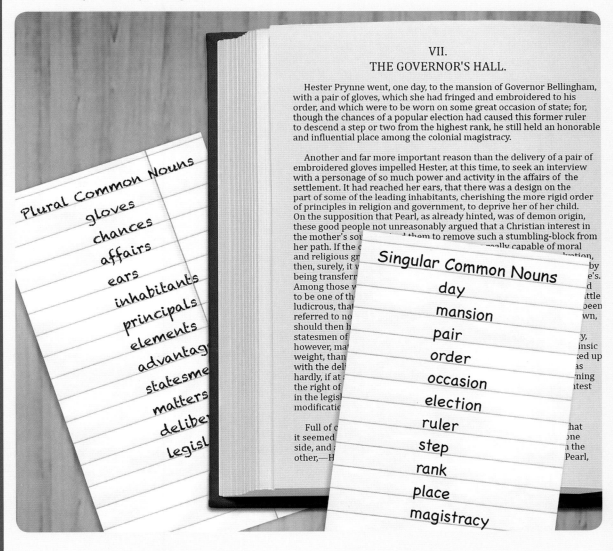

PREP TIME
It might take up to an hour to gather objects, print handouts, and write up center instructions.

Proper Noun Grab Bag
Grades 4-12

Center(s)

Grammar

Skills

Students demonstrate command of the conventions of standard English grammar. More specifically, they practice recognizing the rules for capitalization of proper nouns.

Overview

Students practice identifying proper nouns and preparing to use them in their writing. The tactile and graphic aspects of the activity help make it especially useful for kinesthetic and visual learners. As they consider physical objects and visual cues, students explore aspects of this often misunderstood part of speech.

First, obtain a large bag or box to use as a "grab bag." Collect a variety of items that could be designated as proper nouns. For example: a map with the country, city, or location circled; pictures of famous people; photos of famous buildings; small brand name objects; or excerpts from famous documents or texts. Put about twenty to thirty items in the bag.

ENGAGING™
LEARNERS

Activity Description

Step 1

Members of the group take turns choosing an item from the closed bag.

Step 2

Next, the students identify the proper noun that they've drawn from the bag and explain why it is a proper noun and why it should be capitalized. They can refer to the Proper Noun handout or display.

Step 3

Repeat until the items have all been chosen, identified and explained.

Mini-Lesson

Introduce this activity by reminding the class that nouns are one of the eight parts of speech along with pronouns, verbs, adjectives, adverbs, prepositions, conjunctions, and interjections. Parts of speech indicate how each word functions in meaning as well as grammatically within a sentence.

Although this activity is concerned with proper nouns, this is a good opportunity to explain the difference between common nouns and proper nouns, giving examples of each. (Common nouns begin with a lowercase letter and name non-specific persons, places, things or ideas. Proper nouns begin with an uppercase letter and name a specific person, place, thing or idea.)

Teacher Tips

Instead of giving each student a Proper Noun Handout, you can display a copy of the handout using a projector.

If you have tactile learners be sure to include a large number of 3-dimensional objects in your grab bag.

Center Prep

- A grab bag including a variety of about 30 items that could be designated as proper nouns. (For example: a map with country, city, or location circled; pictures of famous people; photos of famous landmarks; small brand name objects; or excerpts from famous documents or texts. Feel free to adjust the items depending on your content area or unit of study.)
- Proper Noun handout, one for each student
- Written center instructions

Adjusting the Rigor

If students struggle to identify proper nouns, consider expanding the activity. Follow up each proper noun identification by having other students in the group (1) create a sentence using the proper noun, then (2) restating the same sentence but substituting a common noun.

For example: if a Student A pulls out a map with the word Baltimore circled, they will say something like,
"Baltimore is a proper noun because it's the name of a specific city."
Student B will say something like, "Edgar Allan Poe died in Baltimore."
Student C will say, "Edgar Allan Poe died in a city."
This adaptation will reinforce the difference between the specificity of a proper noun and the imprecise meaning of its related common noun.

EXAMPLES OF PROPER NOUNS
Handout

All nouns name a person, place, thing, or idea. But **proper nouns**:
- o name a specific entity.
- o are CAPITALIZED.
- o are usually *not* preceded by an article (a, an, or the)

PERSONS (or pets!)

People's names: Powhatan, George Washington, Kareem Abdul-Jabbar, Mary Todd Lincoln

Pets' names: Fluffy, Rover McDoggy, Mr. Whiskers

Combined titles and names: Mrs. Bennett, Alexander the Great, Dr. Martin Luther King, Jr., President Taft, Lady Jane Grey, General Custer, Principal Skinner, Queen Aminatu

PLACES

Cities, towns, and counties: Denver, Las Vegas, New Delhi, Sault Ste. Marie, Cook County

States, provinces and territories: Idaho, North Carolina, Ontario, Northwest Territories

Countries: Brazil, Central African Republic, United States of America, South Korea

Continents: Africa, South America, Europe, Asia, North America, Antarctica, Austrailia

Bodies of water: Mississippi River, Lake Erie, Pacific Ocean, Caspian Sea, Niagara Falls

Specific geographical locations: Black Forest, Death Valley, Tar-Pamlico River Basin, Rocky Mountains, Mount Kilimanjaro, Matterhorn, Everglades, North Pole

You have permission to reproduce this page for use in your classroom.

ENGAGING™ LEARNERS

EXAMPLES OF PROPER NOUNS
Handout, cont.

THINGS AND IDEAS

Landmarks: Big Ben, White House, Taj Mahal, Hoover Dam, Great Wall of China, Acropolis

Organizations: National Honor Society, American Baseball League, U.S. Navy, Chicago Bulls

Events, battles and wars: Paris Peace Conference, Battle of Gettysburg, Revolutionary War

Brand names: Lego, McDonald's, Kleenex, Subaru Outback, F-16 Fighting Falcon

Months and days: January, May, October, Monday, Thursday, Saturday

Holidays and festivals: Thanksgiving, Jazzfest, Sundance Film Festival, Academy Awards

Eras, periods and civilizations: Precambrian, Jurassic, Stone Age, Nubian Empire, Aztec

Religions and cultural movements: Islam, Sikhism, the Enlightenment, Italian Renaissance

© 2019 Engaging Learners, LLC

Its and It's
Grades 4–12

Center(s)

Grammar

Skills

Students focus on sentence structure and concentrate on the meanings of two common sound-alike words. This simple activity reinforces spelling, grammar, and listening skills.

Overview and Tips for Classroom Implementation

Students draw visual cues to help differentiate between the words *its* and *it's*. Then they listen to a sentence and choose the correct card to complete the sentence. This reinforces understanding of the sentence content while simultaneously giving learners a chance to demonstrate command of two commonly confused words.

Activity Description

Step 1

Draw visual cues

Every member of the group takes a set of cards, one *its* and one *it's*. Ask them to draw a visual cue for themselves so they'll remember which one is which. There is no correct way to do this; each student can choose to copy the cues the teacher demonstrated during the mini-lesson or s/he can do something completely different.

Step 2
Analyze sentences

After they have prepared their visual cues, instruct students to choose sentences, one at a time, from a stack of pre-printed cards or from a worksheet. Tell them to work together to decide whether they'd use *its* or *it's* in each sentence. Encourage them to "think aloud" to explain their reasoning. They should refer to their visual cues – their own or their teammate's – and really think about the meaning of the sentence.

Teacher Tips

It is NOT cheating if students look at other students' visual cues to help them decide which word to use. In fact, you can encourage them to make changes or additions to their own visual cue cards if they find something new.

You can adapt this activity to review other commonly confused words like *your/you're*, *who's/whose*, etc.

As you use this activity more frequently in your classroom, you'll find yourself keeping an eye open for sentences that use the word *its* and *it's* – you'll notice them in textbooks, supplemental texts, and other teaching materials. That will save you some time when you put this activity together.

Students can keep their visual cue cards for later reference or add the words (with hand-drawn cues) to their personal dictionaries.

This center activity was adapted from a popular whole-class activity in which the teacher displays sentences using a projector and students choose the correct index card to hold up in front of their foreheads: *its* or *it's*. After

all students have had practice time in the Literacy & Learning Center, consider using the whole-class activity as a simple, effective, and quick assessment. And if you color-code the *its/it's* cards (by printing *it's* on yellow paper, and *its* on white, for example) you'll be able to see at a glance which students might need extra practice.

Mini-Lesson

Introduce this activity by explaining the difference between the words *its* and *it's*. Remind students that even experienced writers sometimes use the incorrect word. (It's helpful if you can illustrate this by showing an example of an error – a sign, a headline, or even a tweet. Students love seeing adults make mistakes!) Then model drawing a visual cue to help yourself remember the difference between the words. You can draw hands so that the *t* is clutching the *s* to illustrate the possessive nature of *its*, for example. You might want to draw a small *i* under the apostrophe to illustrate that *it's* is a contraction form of *it is*.

Finally, do a "think aloud" so students can hear your reasoning as you choose which word to use. It might sound like this:

> "'*When writing the chemical formula for an ion, <u>its or it's</u> net charge is written in superscript.*' Does the sentence work if I substitute the phrase *it is* for the word *it's*? Let me try it: "When writing the chemical formula for an ion, **it is** net charge is written in superscript." No, that doesn't make any sense. So let's see if one thing belongs to another thing in this sentence…yes! I think the net charge belongs to the ion. Let me read it that way and see if it works. "When writing

135

the chemical formula for an ion, **the net charge that belongs to the ion** is written in superscript." Great! That makes sense! Now let me look at my visual cues to remind myself which version of the word I would use if I wrote this sentence. I like the one where the letter *t* is holding on to the letter *s* because the *s* belongs to it, just like the net charge belongs to the ion."

Remember, by analyzing each sentence closely, your student readers will reinforce their content understanding. You want to encourage that, so be sure to model that thought process.

Adjusting the Rigor

If you have struggling readers in your class, rather than having students take turns reading, you might want to let each group divide into two teams. One team can work together to read a sentence while the other team does the think-aloud and proposes the correct answer. Then they can switch. This way struggling readers will be free to concentrate on the grammar and content rather than stress about the read-aloud aspect.

Students who have already mastered this skill, or who master it quickly, can be invited to take it a step further by writing their own sentences using the words *its* and *it's*. Give them a content-related prompt like, "Write two sentences about Macbeth's first encounter with the witches, one using the word *its* and one using the word *it's*."

Notes

_____

_____

_____

_____

_____

_____

_____

_____

_____

_____

_____

_____

_____

_____

_____

_____

_____

_____

_____

_____

_____

_____

_____

   **ENGAGING™ LEARNERS**

ITS AND IT'S
Example: American History Class (8th Grade)

After noticing his students made a lot of minor grammatical errors in the year's first writing assignment, this teacher incorporated the "Its and It's" Literacy & Learning Center activity into his review of early colonial history. He found some sentences in the text book and on supplemental websites, but he wrote some of them himself.

it's

its

The land in the area wasn't ideal for military settlements because it's/its shallow coastal waters weren't deep enough for warships.

The Roanoke settlement, established in what is now North Carolina, disappeared and it's/its fate is still unknown.

Richard Grenville's original fort was abandoned and it's/its location remains a mystery.

Philip Amadas burned the Aquascogoc village after it's/its residents had been evacuated.

Archeologist excavated parts of what is believed to be a workshop, looking for clues about it's/its size and design.

The legend revolves around the loss of white colonists, but it's/its important to note that many Native Americans also disappeared.

Some researchers believe it's/its likely that stranded colonist were adopted by the friendly Croatoan tribe.

PREP TIME

The first time you use this activity you'll need to print and cut out puzzle pieces, prepare a mini-lesson and write center instructions. The second time you'll only need a few minutes to prepare.

Action Contraction
Grades 4–12

Center(s)

Grammar

Skills

Students practice identifying and constructing contractions. This activity also reinforces close listening skills and speaking in complete sentences.

Overview

Students, especially English Language Learners (ELL), often do not understand that the apostrophe mark in a contraction like *can't* or *wouldn't*, actually signals to the reader that there are letters missing. In this activity, students pair puzzle pieces to identify the source words for common contractions.

Mini-Lesson

Teach or review contractions. Explain how two small words can be "put together" to form another word with an apostrophe representing the missing letters. Model this by saying and writing a few sentences:

"**We are** going to the concert" is the same as "**We're** going to the concert."

"**He's** a brilliant quarterback" is the same as "**He is** a brilliant quarterback."

Invite students to identify the missing letters and point out the apostrophe that is used to replace them.

ENGAGING™
LEARNERS

Center Prep

- Printed and cut-out contraction puzzle pieces (*Tip: You may want to enlarge the photocopy to make the pieces easier to handle.*)
- Timer (optional)
- Written center instructions

Activity Description

Step 1
Instruct students to dump puzzle pieces onto desk/table work surface.

Step 2
Students should take turns putting together puzzle pieces, matching each contraction to its source. As students combine pairs, they should keep their pairs in front of them.

Step 3
After all of the contraction pairs are matched up, students take turns saying a sentence using one of their contractions. Another student has to repeat the sentence using the correct full words.

For example:
Student A says, **"I mustn't** be late for the bus tomorrow."
Student B, who is sitting at Student A's right, says, "I **must not** be late for the bus tomorrow." Then Student B says, "The players from Eastside Prep **aren't** going to win this weekend."
Student C, who is sitting at Student B's right, says, "The players from Eastside Prep **are not** going to win this weekend."

Adjusting the Rigor

To make the activity more rigorous, challenge the students to use their contractions to compose factual sentences based on content material. Other students repeat the factual sentence using full words and then say an additional sentence that builds on or clarifies that fact. For example, in an Earth Science class, Student A might say, "The earth's core **isn't** solid." Student B, who is sitting at Student A's right, could respond with, "The earth's core **is not** solid. It is mostly made up of molten metals." Student B would say, **"You'd** die if you tried to swim to the bottom of the Mariana Trench." Student C, who is sitting at Student B's right, would say, **"You would** die if you tried to swim to the bottom of the Mariana Trench. It's so deep the water pressure would crush your skull."

Notes

_____
_____
_____
_____
_____
_____
_____
_____
_____
_____
_____
_____

ACTION CONTRACTION
Sample Center Instructions

Provide written instructions at the center. Your instructions may look something like this sample. Feel free to adapt this to suit your classroom's needs.

1. **Set up.** Your group has **1 minute** to dump the puzzle pieces out of the basket and put them all right side up.

2. **Make matches**. What words make what contractions? You have 3 minutes to make matches. Take turns! Every student keeps his/her matches.

3. **Say a contraction sentence**. Take turns saying a complete sentence with one of your contractions.

4. **Repeat contraction sentence with full words**. The person next to you repeats your sentence using the full words. Then they say a contraction sentence. Keep taking turns, going around the table, until all contraction pairs have been used in complete sentences.

5. **Clean up.** Put the puzzle pieces back in the basket.

 ENGAGING™ LEARNERS

ACTION CONTRACTION

he's   he has
she is   she's

she'll   she will
he would   he'd

mustn't   must not
might not   mightn't

you've   you have
you would   you'd

we're   we are
I am   I'm

didn't   did not
can not   can't

he'll   he will
could not   couldn't

they're   they are
we will   we'll

aren't   are not
is not   isn't

Notes on this Chapter

Chapter 8
_ _ _ _ _ _ _ _ _ _ _ _ _ _ _ _ _
Tools for Speaking &
Listening Centers

Sentence Starter Discussions
Grades 4–12

Center(s)
Speaking & Listening

Skills
Students practice authentic conversation, using complete sentences and expressing clear thoughts.

Overview
Speaking and listening are the often-neglected aspects of literacy. A Literacy & Learning Center activity like this encourages students to have authentic, engaging discussions, review content, and practice expressing clear thoughts using complete sentences.

Center Prep
- Write three claims about your study topic on colored index cards.
- Print and cut out a set of Sentence Starter cards.
- Timer (optional)
- Written center instructions

Teacher Tips
Keep those sentence starter cards and written activity instructions! You can use them over and over. Next time you do the activity you can just change the claim cards to reflect your current topic of study.

ENGAGING™
LEARNERS

Mini-Lesson

The teacher should model how to use sentence starters before doing this activity the first time.

Activity Description

On colored index cards, write three claims about your study topic. These can be taken from a textbook or supplemental material – or you can make them up yourself. Students choose one claim and comment on it using sentence starter cards as prompts. See this example of claim cards from a high school world history class:

Claim card 1:

During the Renaissance, improved map making and shipbuilding contributed to expanding trade. This resulted in a burst of economic growth throughout Europe.

Claim card 2:

When we think of 15th century Florence today, we think of painters, architects, and writers. But in reality, bankers and guilds were responsible for the city's growth.

Claim card 3:

The common people, who lived in Europe during this period, weren't greatly affected by the Renaissance. They still spent their days struggling to find adequate food and avoid illness and injury.

Adjusting the Rigor

After students have mastered Sentence Starter Discussions, you can add another step. Upon completion of the activity, let the students take turns reflecting on the activity using one of the following questions as a prompt. They should be encouraged to use their own words. They don't need sentence starters for this part of the activity.

- What one new thing did I learn during this conversation?

- Did I hear anything that made me see things in a new way or change my opinion?

- Did I express myself clearly?

- Did everyone understand me?

- Did I understand all of my groupmates' sentences? (If not, ask him/her to re-state it – and listen more closely this time. If you still don't understand, ask him/her to clarify. Work as a team to figure out the best way to say it.)

- If I could go back and say one of my sentences again, what would I change to make it clearer?

SENTENCE STARTER DISCUSSIONS
Sample Center Instructions

Provide written instructions at the center. Your instructions may look something like this sample. Feel free to adapt this to suit your classroom's needs.

1.   **Select a claim card** for discussion. You have two minutes to read each of the claim cards aloud and select one card for discussion.

Discuss the claim.

2.   Everyone quickly **select a sentence starter card.**

3.   Go around the table giving everyone a chance to **say** their sentence about the claim. **Listen** closely to what everyone says!

4.   **Swap** sentence starter cards with another member of your group.

5.   **Repeat** the activity, making sure you don't say the same thing that your groupmate said. Say something new!

ENGAGING™ LEARNERS

SENTENCE STARTER CARD

SENTENCE STARTER CARD

I see it differently because....

SENTENCE STARTER CARD

This suggests that....

SENTENCE STARTER CARD

An example of this is....

SENTENCE STARTER CARD

Put another way, the claim is stating....

SENTENCE STARTER CARD

I agree with the claim because....

SENTENCE STARTER CARD

The point about ... is important because ....

SENTENCE STARTER CARD

Despite agreeing with..., I disagree that....

SENTENCE STARTER CARD

I agree, and....

You have permission to reproduce this page for use in your classroom.

PREP TIME
You'll need to invest a little time to prepare a discussion activity that's relevant to your content - but it's worth it. Allow yourself time to write a resolution, new information cards, and discussion prompts.

Changing Your Mind
Grades 4–12

Center(s)
Speaking & Listening

Skills
Students are given a chance to self-reflect on a Resolution and form a personal opinion: Strongly Agree, Agree, Disagree, or Strongly Disagree. Then, as a series of New Information cards are read aloud, students are invited to re-examine their opinion and change their mind. This is an adaptation of the Four Corners Debate activity in which students move to different corners of the room to indicate their changing opinions.

Overview
This activity may take more than one center rotation to complete. You might want to set up your centers so that the Changing Your Mind center is followed by a Teacher-Led center. There's usually a lot to discuss and teacher guidance and assessment is valuable.

Center Prep
- 1 Resolution card per center
- 3–8 New Information cards per center
- 1 set of Personal Opinion cards per student
- 2 Discussion Prompts per center
- Written center instructions

See the Resolution and New Information card examples at the end of this activity.

Activity Description

Step 1
Consider the Resolution

One student reads the Resolution Card aloud. Students have 1 minute to consider what they know about the topic and how their personal experiences might relate to the resolution. Then they pick up a Personal Decision card that says either, *Strongly Agree*, *Agree*, *Disagree* or *Strongly Disagree*.

Step 2
Consider New Information

Students take turns reading new information cards aloud. After each fact is introduced, the group has a minute or two to discuss its implications. Then the students take a moment to silently consider how the new fact affects their personal opinion. They then can change their opinion by putting down their Personal Decision card and picking up a different one.

Step 3
Discuss the Results

Students can do this in their center groups, with the teacher in a teacher-led center, or as part of a follow-up full class activity. Give the students a choice of prompts to help guide the conversation.

Examples of discussion prompts might include:

- Did your opinion change as you learned new information? Why?

- What thoughts went through your head during the self-reflection moments? Give examples.

- Did your team members' decisions ever affect your decisions? How?

- Which new information was the most interesting? Did it encourage you to rethink your previous position or did it reinforce your previous position?

- Did the source of the new information make any difference to you? Which sources seemed more reliable? How do we know if a source is reliable?

- Did any of the new information seem to be deliberately appealing to your emotions rather than your reason? Which emotion do you think it was it trying to trigger: fear, anger, self-satisfaction, a sense of well being, etc.? Did it work?

- Did you notice any obvious fallacies? Start by looking for exaggerations. When speakers and writers use words like *always*, *never*, *must*, *all* or *none*, there's a chance they're exaggerating.

- If people have different opinions when they first hear a premise, can we expect them to agree with each other after they've learned new information? Why or why not?

Teacher Tips

This activity can be set up so that each center has a different Resolution and a different set of New Information cards. Student teams can then rotate from center to center. The Teacher-Led center can be positioned after any one of the centers. Other teams can discuss prompts themselves while the one team reflects with the teacher.

The resolution and new information don't have to be written on cards. They can be on slips of paper, digital files, whatever works for your classroom.

Mini-Lesson

Changing your mind when you encounter new information is a sign of strength, not weakness. It means you're thinking. And sometimes, even after you've looked at the facts, you're still undecided. Big questions often don't have simple yes or no answers. Two smart people can both be "right" and still disagree. Thanks to the scientific method – and thanks to historians, scientists, and researchers of all kinds, we're always getting more facts, more data, and more details to inform our decision-making.

There are three concrete steps we can take to help us make informed decisions:

Concrete Step 1

When you encounter new information, consider the source.

Think about the differences between well-researched studies that are trying to inform you and opinion pieces that are trying to manipulate you. Sometimes other people's opinions can be disguised as facts. Sometimes studies are flawed. Sometimes things that are presented as facts are, in fact, based on fallacies. But many times new information is actually valuable. It can inspire us to change our mind, reinforce opinions we already have, or make us look at things in a new way.

Concrete Step 2

Consider your emotions but don't be ruled by them.

Sometimes when we consider a new idea, we can't help but feel angry or fearful. We all want to be comfortable so don't ignore your feelings. Instead, take some time to self-reflect and think about why you have those feelings. Is the perceived threat real? What is the difference between a dangerous thought and an uncomfortable thought? Could a new idea and your comfortable worldview actually co-exist side-by-side?

Concrete Step 3

Be aware of how peers might be affecting your reasoning.

Sometimes we want to agree with others simply because we want them to think highly of us. Everyone wants friends. Sometimes we want to disagree with others simply because we want to be different. We all want to be unique. Don't ignore either of these impulses, but realize that they might be affecting your decision-making. A safe classroom situation like this is a good time to experiment with trusting your own reasoning powers.

Notes
_____
_____
_____
_____
_____
_____
_____
_____
_____

ENGAGING™ LEARNERS

Adjusting the Rigor

This lesson encapsulates a whole undergraduate degree worth of education so you'll probably need to simplify it for your grade 4-12 students! I recommend using the mini-lesson to focus on ONE of the concrete steps when you first introduce the activity. Then, every time you use the activity, you can add another. Build your students' reasoning power, aiming toward the day when they will be independently able to recognize and incorporate all of the considerations involved in rational decision-making.

For the lower grades, you could break the three concrete steps down even further. Focus only on identifying the central idea of each new information card, recognizing one kind of fallacy, or discerning between reliable and unreliable sources, for example. Some textbooks offer sample arguments for in-class debates and discussions. They are great sources for Resolution and New Information cards. Or check out these websites:
https://www.procon.org/
https://www.intelligencesquaredus.org/

CHANGING YOUR MIND
Sample Center Instructions

Provide written instructions at the center. Your instructions may look something like this sample.
Feel free to adapt this to suit your classroom's needs.

1. Choose one team member to tread the Resolution card aloud. Discuss it, if necessary, and make sure all members of your group understand it.

2. Think quietly to yourself. Do you agree or disagree with the resolution? After 1 minute, put a Personal Opinion card down, face up so everyone can see.

3. Choose a team member to read one New Information card aloud. Make sure all the members of your group understand it.

4. Think quietly to yourself. Now that you have this new information do you still have the same opinion? After 1 minute, change your Personal Opinion card if you want.

5. Repeat steps 3 and 4 until all the New Information cards have been read.

6. Turn over the two Discussion Prompt cards, read them aloud, and choose one prompt to inspire your discussion. You have 5 mins. for a group discussion. Everyone should participate.

CHANGING YOUR MIND
Example: Social Studies (4th Grade)

The teacher interviewed members of the school community to get quotes and used the Changing Your Mind center activity during a unit on civic responsibility.

RESOLUTION CARD

Woodland Middle School should be run like a democracy with students being allowed to vote on everything.

NEW INFORMATION CARDS:

Citizenship is a balance of privileges and responsibilities. I suspect students would like the privilege of deciding things, but they wouldn't welcome the responsibilities that go along with it.
– Mr. Soto (Assistant Principal)

Even in representative democracies like the United States, the citizens don't vote on *everything*. Citizens have to trust their representatives to make good decisions, just like Woodland students have to trust their teachers.
– Mrs. Leacock (Teacher)

It would have been better if I had more say in what happened in middle school because when I started in high school I didn't even know what extracurriculars to pick.
– Javier Vargas (Westmont High football team)

The trouble...is that we have taken our democracy for granted; we have thought and acted as if our forefathers had founded it once and for all. We have forgotten that it has to be enacted anew in every generation.
– John Dewey (American philosopher and educator)

I think if we voted on things the bullies would just make everybody do what they wanted.
– anonymous (4th grade student)

DISCUSSION PROMPT CARD

How might your opinion have been different if the premise said, "Woodland Middle School should be run like a democracy with students being allowed to vote on **some** things"?

Did all sources seem equally reliable and important? Why or why not?

CHANGING YOUR MIND
Example: Advanced Biology (11ᵗʰ Grade)

The teacher researched the topic on **www.procon.org** and used the Changing Your Mind center activity as an introduction to the dissection unit.

RESOLUTION CARD

Laboratories should have the right to use live animals for medical or commercial testing.

NEW INFORMATION CARDS:

The American Heart Association stated in its "Public Policy Agenda 2010-14," available at heart.org, (accessed Oct. 29, 2013): "Animal research has improved the health and welfare of animals and humans. The decline in death rates in the United States from heart disease and stroke since the 1960s is due to lifestyle changes and new methods of treatment and prevention, many of which are based on animal research."

In Defense of Animals (IDA), an international animal rights and rescue organization, stated in its article titled "Responsible Research," posted on its website (accessed Oct. 24, 2013): "It is possible, in the twenty-first century, to conduct a vast array of experiments without using animals and to derive better results more quickly and at less cost. Cutting-edge technology has forged new frontiers with the use of lasers, fiber optics, microchips, genomics, computer-based drug design, and digital imaging, to name a few.

Jane Goodall, PhD, ethologist and author, stated in her Mar. 17, 2012 op-ed for the Times (UK) titled "So Much Animal Pain, So Little Human Gain": "Animal experimenters often justify such research by claiming the existence in humans of some morally relevant characteristics, such as intelligence, language, or consciousness, that are supposedly absent in other species. But we are fast discovering a great deal about high levels of intelligence in many animal species, and too about animal consciousness, emotions and sensitivity to pain."

Dario L. Ringach, PhD, MSc, Professor of Neurobiology and Psychology at the University of California at Los Angeles, stated in his article titled "The Use of Nonhuman Animals in Biomedical Research," published in the Oct. 2011 issue of the American Journal of the Medical Sciences: "Why is the use of animals in scientific experimentation morally permissible? In my view, it is because the moral status of animals is not equal to that of humans and because opting out of the research condemns our patients (both animal and human) to suffer and die of disease."

DISCUSSION PROMPT CARD

Choose one question to discuss.
(1) Did any of the new information seem to be deliberately appealing to your emotions rather than your reason? Give examples.
(2) What thoughts went through your head during the self-reflection moments? Give examples.

CHANGING YOUR MIND
Example: Science (6th Grade)

A teacher found this premise and new information on
https://www.intelligencesquaredus.org/debates/genetically-modify-food

---

RESOLUTION CARD

Woodland Middle School
should be run like a democracy
with students being allowed to
vote on everything.

NEW INFORMATION CARDS:

Citizenship is a balance of privileges and responsibilities. I suspect students would like the privilege of deciding things, but they wouldn't welcome the responsibilities that go along with it.
– Mr. Soto (Assistant Principal)

Even in representative democracies like the United States, the citizens don't vote on *everything*. Citizens have to trust their representatives to make good decisions, just like Woodland students have to trust their teachers.
– Mrs. Leacock (Teacher)

It would have been better if I had more say in what happened in middle school because when I started in high school I didn't even know what extracurriculars to pick.
– Javier Vargas
(Westmont High football team)

The trouble...is that we have taken our democracy for granted; we have thought and acted as if our forefathers had founded it once and for all. We have forgotten that it has to be enacted anew in every generation.
– John Dewey
(American philosopher and educator)

I think if we voted on things the bullies would just make everybody do what they wanted.
– anonymous (4th grade student)

DISCUSSION PROMPT CARD

How might your opinion have been different if the premise said, "Woodland Middle School should be run like a democracy with students being allowed to vote on **some** things"?

Did all sources seem equally reliable and important? Why or why not?

**ENGAGING™
LEARNERS**

CHANGING YOUR MIND

AGREE	STRONGLY DISAGREE
STRONGLY AGREE	DISAGREE

You have permission to reproduce this page for use in your classroom.

True False Reasoning
Grades 4-12

Center(s)
Speaking & Listening
Reading Together

Skills
Students practice reading, reasoning, citing evidence, conversation, and persuasion, while reviewing content.

Overview
This activity is a good way to repurpose true/false worksheets and quizzes. Students take turns reading true/false content-review statements aloud. The group has to discuss why they believe each statement is true or false.

Mini-Lesson
Model this activity and do some practice rounds as part of whole group instruction. Demonstrate how to cite evidence (show the source for evidence by mentioning the page or chapter number) and how to explain reasoning by describing your thought process step by step.

Center Prep
- True/false questions written on individual index cards or slips of paper
- Answer key (optional)
- Timer (optional)
- Written center instructions

Teacher Tips

Students tend to want to say the correct statement as evidence that an answer is false. Emphasize that saying the true answer is NOT the same as explaining why an answer is false. Students need to explain their reasoning. For example, if the statement is, "Comets in the Kuiper Belt are not part of the solar system," students can't just say, "Oh yes they are!" Instead, they need to explain their reasoning or cite a source by saying something like, "The illustration on page 470 shows that those comets are part of the solar system," or "Comets in the Kuiper belt obey the same laws of motion as planets and their moons, and they are made of the same stuff as planets and moons."

Give students an idea of how long each question should take. They might get bogged down on one or two questions. Encourage them to move forward, allowing no more than a minute or two for each explanation.

Notes

_____
_____
_____
_____
_____
_____
_____
_____
_____
_____

TRUE FALSE REASONING
Sample Center Instructions

Provide written instructions at the center. Your instructions may look something like this sample. Feel free to adapt this to suit your classroom's needs.

1. Take turns being the reader.

2. The reader has to take a card and read the statement aloud.

3. The rest of the team has to decide if the statement is true or false. Take turns explaining your reasoning and citing your evidence.

4. You have 8 true/false statements to cover in 10 minutes! Pace yourselves and don't waste time.

5. Spend the last 2 minutes of looking at the answer key. How did your team do? Did you get most of them right?

6. Think about the difference between good reasoning and sloppy reasoning. We'll discuss this as a class after we're done with centers today.

PREP TIME
Use this center activity as a way to re-purpose existing multiple-choice quizzes or worksheets. Allow time to write up center instructions and prepare for mini-lesson.

Multiple Choice Reasoning
Grades 4-12

Center(s)
Speaking & Listening
Reading Together

Skills
Students practice reading, reasoning, citing evidence, conversation, and persuasion, while reviewing content.

Overview
This activity is a good way to repurpose multiple choice worksheets and quizzes. Students take turns reading multiple-choice, content-review questions aloud. The group has to discuss why they believe each answer is correct or incorrect.

Mini-Lesson
Model this activity and do some practice rounds as part of whole group instruction. Demonstrate how to cite evidence (show the source for evidence by mentioning the page or chapter number) and how to explain reasoning by describing your thought process step by step.

Center Prep
- Multiple-choice questions written on individual index cards or slips of paper
- Answer key (optional)
- Timer (optional)
- Written center instructions

  ENGAGING™ LEARNERS

Teacher Tips

Students tend to want to say the correct answer as evidence that an answer is incorrect. Emphasize that saying the correct answer is NOT the same as explaining why an answer is incorrect. Students need to explain their reasoning. For example, if the question is, "What US city sits at a latitude of about 30 degrees north and a longitude of about 90 degrees west?" and the students are asked to consider Los Angeles, CA, they can't just say, "New Orleans would be the right answer!" Instead, they need to explain their reasoning by saying something like, "I remember that here in Oklahoma City we're about 35, -97. So the correct city would have to be south and east of us. Los Angeles is west of us, so this can't be right."

Give students an idea of how long each question should take. Encourage them to move forward, allowing no more than a minute or two for each explanation.

Notes

_____
_____
_____
_____
_____
_____
_____
_____
_____
_____
_____

MULTIPLE CHOICE REASONING
Sample Center Instructions

Provide written instructions at the center. Your instructions may look something like this sample. Feel free to adapt this to suit your classroom's needs.

1. Take turns being the reader.

2. The reader has to take a card and read the question aloud. Then they read each possible answer one at a time.

3. The rest of the team has to decide if each answer is correct or not. Take turns explaining your reasoning and citing your evidence.

4. You have 5 multiple choice questions to cover in 10 minutes! Pace yourselves and don't waste time.

5. Spend the last 2 minutes of looking at the answer key. How did your team do? Did you get most of them right?

6. Think about the difference between good reasoning and sloppy reasoning. If you know some facts or information, does that makes it easier to "guess" the correct answer? We'll discuss this as a class after we're done with centers today.

Elements of an Argument
Grades 4–12

Center(s)

Speaking & Listening

Skills

Students practice identifying claims and recognizing supporting facts in either written texts or oral (spoken-word) presentations.

Overview

It has been said that students have to recognize arguments before they can be expected to make arguments. In this activity, students begin by engaging in close reading or attentive listening. Then they complete a graphic organizer by identifying the author or speaker's claim, supporting facts, and/or premises.

Teacher Tips

It's important for students to gain experience listening to arguments as well as reading them. But sometimes it's difficult to find relevant, age-appropriate examples of spoken arguments that relate to your content. If you can't find any, consider recording your own. Read passages from the textbook or supplemental reading material aloud. Students can listen to the recordings at the Literacy & Learning Center.

Mini-Lesson

Model the activity using a separate printed or recorded passage. Remind students that the ability to identify and then address the other side's claims and supporting facts is an important step in winning any debate. Adolescents love to argue, so they're likely to respond positively.

Center Prep

- A printed or recorded (depending on if you want a reading or listening activity) passage that consists of one claim and a few supporting facts.
- Print the Elements of an Argument graphic organizers. Print enough copies so that each student will have a choice of which organizer to use.
- Writing implements (pens, pencils)
- Timer (optional)
- Written center instructions

Adjusting the Rigor

Challenge students to identify the claim and supporting facts without the use of a graphic organizer. They can record their findings in an outline form or as simple notations.

Notes

_____

_____

_____

_____

_____

_____

_____

ELEMENTS OF AN ARGUMENT
Sample Center Instructions

Provide written instructions at the center. Your instructions may look something like this sample. Feel free to adapt this to suit your classroom's needs.

1. Listen closely to the recording. (2 minutes)

2. Work as a team to identify the speaker's claim. (What do they want you to believe?) What facts do they offer to support their claim? You can listen to the recording as many times as you need to. (6 minutes)

3. Individually choose a graphic organizer and fill in the claim and supporting facts. (6 minutes)

4. Bring your completed graphic organizer to the Teacher-Led Center. We'll discuss your work.

ELEMENTS OF AN ARGUMENT
Graphic Organizer 1

Name _____ Date _____

Who is talking? _____

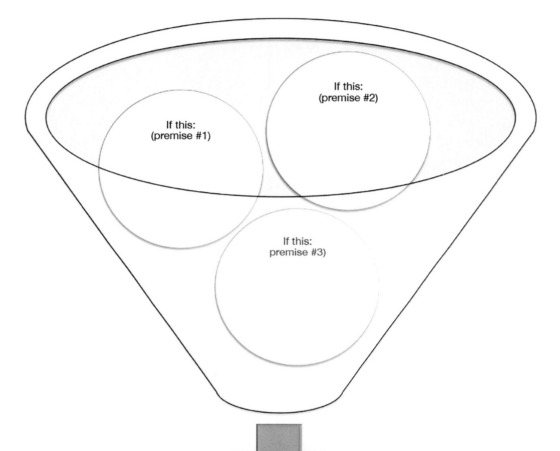

If this:
(premise #1)

If this:
(premise #2)

If this:
premise #3)

Then you are expected to believe this:

Write the claim in your own words here:

ENGAGING™ LEARNERS

ELEMENTS OF AN ARGUMENT
Graphic Organizer 2

Name _____ Date _____

Who is talking? _____

In this passage, a person is making a claim and supporting it with facts. Record the claim and the supporting facts in the boxes. **Write them in your own words.**

Supporting fact

+

Supporting fact

+

Claim

⟷

Supporting fact

+

Supporting fact

ELEMENTS OF AN ARGUMENT
Graphic Organizer 1 Example

Name _Terri Cruz_ Date _11/19/15_

Who is talking? _Collin O'Mara - President & CEO of National Wildlife Federation_

Source: www.NWF.org "The Gulf Has Waited Long Enough"

If this:
(premise #1)

Courts have found BP's actions grossly negligent.

If this:
(premise #2)

Many wildlife species have been negatively impacted.

If this:
premise #3)

BP put profits ahead of safety.

Then you are expected to believe this:

Write the claim in your own words here:

BP has been found guilty so we should get the money and start cleaning up the mess they made!

ENGAGING™
LEARNERS

ELEMENTS OF AN ARGUMENT
Graphic Organizer 2 Example

Name __Paul Midlum__   Date __4/2/16__

Who is talking? __American History textbook - chapter 9__

In this passage, a person is making a claim and supporting it with facts. Record the claim and the supporting facts in the boxes. **Write them in your own words.**

Supporting fact

Deficits increased under Hoover.

Supporting fact

He championed central planning of the economy.

Claim

Herbert Hoover was NOT laissez-faire.

Supporting fact

Federal spending increased 1929-1932.

Supporting fact

He asked business leaders to keep wages high as the economy fell.

Notes on this Chapter

Conclusion

The Courage to Build a
Powerful Learning Community

The Courage to Build a Powerful Learning Community

It takes courage to change practice. Fortunately, I know that our profession is made up of brave individuals. We know that if we're going to create the classrooms that our students need, there's simply no place for comments like "I've always done it this way" or "but I have to get ready for the test."

As I have worked with educators in varied school contexts, I have discovered the following about Literacy & Learning Centers:

1. Students positively respond to them

2. Test scores go up

3. Discipline challenges in the classroom and within the school go down

4. Students and teachers indicate that time passes quickly in class. That's especially exciting since that's an indicator that the students and teachers are in the psychological state of "flow" (Csikszentmihalyi, 2014)

You have the power to make this happen in your classroom.

As I mentioned in Chapter 2, the strategies in this book can be used as part of the Literacy & Learning Center model or not. As quick "fill ins" or on days when you aren't using centers, you can teach the mini-lesson and then adapt the activities for full-class, small group, or independent student work. Regardless of how you use these activities, their

focus is to provide students with ample opportunities to practice key literacy skills. And, because content study is the ideal way to develop literacy skills, they are specifically designed to work within the content areas/ disciplines. But make no mistake; the Literacy & Learning Center model is the ideal way to do this. It maximizes instructional time and is thus able to provide the greatest opportunity for student practice.

If you want to learn more about getting started with Literacy & Learning Center model, visit our website engaginglearners. com/literacy-learning-centers. And for more information about the research that led to the development of the model, and teacher tips for implementation, read the book, *Literacy and Learning Centers for the Big Kids: Building Literacy Skills and Content Knowledge, Grades 4–12.*

Thank you for all you do for students,

Katie McKnight

References

Csikszentmihalyi, M. (2014). Applications of *Flow in Human Development and Education: The Collected Works of Mihaly Csikszentmihalyi.* Dordrecht: Springer, 2014.

Notes on this Book

Notes on this Book, Cont.

Want more classroom activities?

Subscribe to
EngagingLearners.com/tools
for tools, teacher tips, and classroom activities to
develop literacy skills and content knowledge

It's your source for lessons that have been specifically
adapted to the Literacy & Learning Center model.

Try it FREE for two weeks!

Then use **discount code LLCVOL1** to receive **50% off** an annual
subscription. Contact info@engaginglearners.com for details on group
discounts for school districts.